I0459494

# The Voice
# of Genius is Soft

# The Voice of Genius is Soft

An Annotated Autobiography of A Psychoanalyst

*Peter D. King, M.D., Ph.D.*

*Edited by Simone M. King*
*And*
*Tom King*

**LitPrime**
*"Your story is our priority"*

LitPrime Solutions
21250 Hawthorne Blvd
Suite 500, Torrance, CA 90503
www.litprime.com
Phone: 1-800-981-9893

© 2023 Peter D. King, M.D., Ph.D. All rights reserved.

No part of this book may be reproduced, stored in a retrieval system, or transmitted by any means without the written permission of the author.

Published by LitPrime Solutions    05/04/2023

ISBN: 979-8-88703-207-8(sc)
ISBN: 979-8-88703-208-5(e)

Library of Congress Control Number: 2023905200

Any people depicted in stock imagery provided by iStock are models, and such images are being used for illustrative purposes only.

Certain stock imagery © iStock.

Because of the dynamic nature of the Internet, any web addresses or links contained in this book may have changed since publication and may no longer be valid. The views expressed in this work are solely those of the author and do not necessarily reflect the views of the publisher, and the publisher hereby disclaims any responsibility for them.

# CONTENTS

Foreword By Simone M. King . . . . . . . . . . . . . . . . . . . . . . . . . . .vii

Foreword By Tom King . . . . . . . . . . . . . . . . . . . . . . . . . . . . . xiii

Preface By Mark Fisher, M.D. . . . . . . . . . . . . . . . . . . . . . . . .xv

Foreword Notes from the Couch By Ria Parody Erlich . . . . . . .xvii

Acknowledgments . . . . . . . . . . . . . . . . . . . . . . . . . . . . . . xxi

Preface . . . . . . . . . . . . . . . . . . . . . . . . . . . . . . . . . . . . . .xxv


Chapter I.  Introduction . . . . . . . . . . . . . . . . . . . . . . . . . 1

Chapter II.  Professional Ideas and Musings . . . . . . . . . . . . . . . .12

    Schizophrenia . . . . . . . . . . . . . . . . . . . . . . . . . . . . . . .12

    The Principle of Truth . . . . . . . . . . . . . . . . . . . . . . . . . .18

    Cosmon, Anti-Cosmon, and Parity in the Universe . . . . . . . 20

    Bonding Dissonance and Schizophrenia . . . . . . . . . . . . . . .21

    Bonding Dissonance and Infantile Autism . . . . . . . . . . . . . .23

    Brain Changes as a Result of Experience . . . . . . . . . . . . . . .25

    Altruism as a Basic Drive . . . . . . . . . . . . . . . . . . . . . . . .32

    Completion and Credit as Basic Needs . . . . . . . . . . . . . . . .33

    The Relativity of Time and the King Postulate . . . . . . . . . .39

    King Arthur's Sword . . . . . . . . . . . . . . . . . . . . . . . . . . .41

Chapter III.  Beginnings . . . . . . . . . . . . . . . . . . . . . . . . . 46

Chapter IV.  A Little About Sex . . . . . . . . . . . . . . . . . . . . . . .61

Chapter V.  Early Youth . . . . . . . . . . . . . . . . . . . . . . . . . .69

Early Thoughts . . . . . . . . . . . . . . . . . . . . . . . . . . . . . . . .69
Serving Our Country . . . . . . . . . . . . . . . . . . . . . . . . . . .72
Chapter VI. God, Poetry and Other Ideas . . . . . . . . . . . . . . . . .76
God and Religion . . . . . . . . . . . . . . . . . . . . . . . . . . . . . . .76
Natural Authority . . . . . . . . . . . . . . . . . . . . . . . . . . . . . . 77
Communication . . . . . . . . . . . . . . . . . . . . . . . . . . . . . . .79
Poetry and Beauty . . . . . . . . . . . . . . . . . . . . . . . . . . . . . 90
Some More Creative Thoughts . . . . . . . . . . . . . . . . . . . . .95
Chapter VII. Macho Power . . . . . . . . . . . . . . . . . . . . . . . . . . . 99
Chapter VIII. The Athlete . . . . . . . . . . . . . . . . . . . . . . . . . . .109
Chapter IX. Heritage And Money . . . . . . . . . . . . . . . . . . . .119
Heritage . . . . . . . . . . . . . . . . . . . . . . . . . . . . . . . . . . . .119
Money . . . . . . . . . . . . . . . . . . . . . . . . . . . . . . . . . . . . . .123
Chapter X. The Psychiatrist . . . . . . . . . . . . . . . . . . . . . . . .127
Chapter XI. Conclusion . . . . . . . . . . . . . . . . . . . . . . . . . . .158
A Unified Theory of Human Behavior
Explaining All Psychiatric Symptoms . . . . . . . . . . . . . . . . .163

Bibliography . . . . . . . . . . . . . . . . . . . . . . . . . . . . . . . . . . . .171
About the Author . . . . . . . . . . . . . . . . . . . . . . . . . . . . . . . .177

# FOREWORD

## By Simone M. King

The death of my husband, Dr. Peter D. King, was the final beat of a once strong heart. Like life itself, he had been constantly in motion. But suddenly and unexpectedly, on August 28, 2000, all movement stopped.

I felt as if I had been thrown from a cliff and that my life, too, had ended. After all, Peter and I had known each other for twenty-eight years and had been married for twenty-six.

In my desperation, I imagined myself in his death cave, searching for something to substitute for his real physical attributes – how he sounded, smelled and tasted through my five senses. I wanted to follow him and would have if I could. We had promised to go on life's journey together, through pleasure, pain, joy and sorrow, but now he had left me here alone. We never even had the chance to say goodbye.

During the time we had together, Peter spoke and wrote about myriad far-reaching and universal subjects – everything from psychiatry, teaching and research to government, philosophy, society and the search for truth. At the time of his death, he was writing a book that contained not only his collected ideas and theories, but also extensive material on how they had been informed by his life experiences. He called the book *The Voice of Genius Is Soft [An Annotated Autobiography of a Psychoanalyst]*.

As soon as Peter's colleagues, family, friends and patients urged me to get his book published, I realized that his writings were a tangible part of himself that he had left behind. I discovered that while reading his words, I felt almost as if I were with him again and sharing his life. Also, it became a therapeutic, healing experience for me.

Peter's love of life and zest for living inspired me to restart my own life, and the more I read it, the more I felt my love for him compelling me to publish his book – on the one hand, as he might have said. On the other hand, he would have continued, maybe I'm doing it because I'm still living under the spell of his power and am a prisoner of his love.

I felt that I was meeting Peter again as I read his writings and reacquainted myself with his philosophies that demonstrated so concisely methods all of us can use to help us relish every moment of our lives. He seemed always to be searching for even the smallest action or detail that might make life better and possibly prolong it.

Peter's own life was filled with family, colleagues, patients, work, ambitions, explorations, music, poetry and writing, as well as other vital pursuits too numerous to mention and lots of love. His personality was magnetic. Once people got to know him, they could not help but like him.

Peter was devoted to the ideals of goodness, fairness and freedom of individual expression and thought, as well as accuracy, hard work and self-discipline without compromise. He also held fast to everything that he believed was inspirational, positive, promising and right.

Peter's energy was bountiful and seemingly limitless. He himself led a "blue-jeans and tuxedo" lifestyle that reflected both his work ethic and his belief in getting the most pleasure possible from life. He published fifty papers in the field of medicine, including works on autism, schizophrenia and related issues, many of which contained findings that were ahead of their time. He also found time to maintain his private practice, to travel the world and to design and build "King's Court," a housing community on eighteen acres in the Bel Air section of Los Angeles that contained our personal French chateau.

For Peter, emotional and physical fitness went hand in hand, and he practiced what he preached. He was a bodybuilder, marathon runner and triathlete, who won first place in his age group in the 1983 Long Beach Triathlon. He also encouraged me – as he did everyone – to build my "mental muscles," which he called "emotional muscle building," so that I would be psychologically fit as well, which, I confess, helped me tremendously during times of stress in our marriage. For twenty-six years we stood on a strong foundation of love, but sometimes issues of how to raise our children or establish a moral standard for them caused earthquakes in our relationship, during which we could and would erupt like volcanoes and roar like thunder. In other words, we both got hot under the collar.

Typically, I allowed my instincts and intuition to be defeated by the weight of his persuasive powers and professional right to say he was right!

Maybe it was because of our cultural differences. As a Korean-American, I come from a culture that defers to the wisdom of age (Peter was ten years older than I), education and gender. Of course, I genuinely respected Peter's experience and authority, but often discounted myself in the process and did not always speak up when he told our children that he was better informed than I and that they should follow his advice and not mine. (I've grown less concerned about offering my opinion in the thirty-six years that I've lived in this country, but I feel I still have what I call an "Asian silhouette" that sometimes still makes me feel shy. However, that's another book for another time.)

Most of the time, Peter would skillfully apply his professional talents to the situation, and our arguments would last less than five minutes. He would win back my heart with loving gestures and magic words, and I would deal with any residual anger by channeling my energy into my paintings or running.

Sometimes, however, my anger and emotions could not be stopped from boiling over. Being an inveterate problem solver, Peter, to his credit, was always willing to work as hard as necessary on resolving the issues between us. He had a special knack for doing it in a way that was humorous and playful and that could transform the mood of the moment from angry and chaotic to calm and pleasant, which, for me, evoked the feeling of listening to a beautiful composition by Mozart – but without the music.

Here's an example: After one of our classic battles, I asked Peter to be my psychiatrist instead of my husband, to "mirror" himself. He agreed. I began to complain bitterly and profusely to "Dr. King" about "Peter." The look on Dr. King's/Peter's face suggested to me that he hadn't fully realized how serious the issues were from my point of view.

Finally, he stopped my outburst by saying, "Your husband sounds like a jerk! Of course you need your space and freedom. He shouldn't be so critical of you and interfere in your domain. As your metaphor implies, you felt like he was choking you, like a leash pulled tight around a dog's neck. He has a bad spirit to do that, especially since he's in love with you."

Then, barely suppressing a smile, he asked, "Shall we end this session?"

Before we married, Peter and I attended a party at the home of our good friend Bill Desmond Ryan, president of Royal Hawaiian Investment Company, and his wife Jackie. When we told them of our plans to marry, Bill, for some reason, earnestly and vigorously tried to talk us out of it. Peter stood his ground and remained firm with Bill, but at the same time, feeling nervous that he might lose me because of what Bill had said, treated me all evening as if his feet were on thin ice.

Bill must have sensed what was happening, because he eventually came over to me, got down on his knees in front of us, held and kissed my hand and said to me, "I honor Peter's love for you."

And that's exactly how I felt, no matter how many arguments we got into, and in spite of the occasional complaint about me in Peter's book. Peter always honored our love for each other.

My husband, Dr. Peter D. King, lived his life humbly, but fully. I dare say he achieved most, if not all, of his personal and professional goals.

As the music of Mozart heals my spirit, so too, do Peter's writings encourage me to continue to pursue the best possible quality of life. I want to share his gifts with you, the reader, in the hope that you will conclude, as he did, that we all have "the voice of genius."

*Simone M. King August 2002*

# FOREWORD

## BY TOM KING

My brother, Dr. Peter D. King, wrote this book, *THE VOICE OF GENIUS IS SOFT [An Annotated Autobiography of a Psychoanalyst]*, during the last several years of his life, just before he succumbed to liver cancer. Peter slipped into a coma unexpectedly while recovering from a liver operation in the Kaiser Foundation Hospital in Los Angeles and died on August 28, 2000, to the great sadness of us all — his family, friends, patients and professional colleagues. His widow, Simone Mi Sook King, has wished to proceed with the book's publication for a number of personal reasons. Principally, she knows that Peter would want it to be published and made available to the medical community and to the wider reading public.

Being an autobiography, the book provides a number of facts regarding Peter's development from babyhood into his adult years. Peter presents these facts in a unique and fascinating manner. All through his life, he applied his keen intelligence and rich imagination to a great variety of religious, philosophic and scientific problems. He formulated many of his ideas into Postulates and Theories. In this book, Peter weaves the conclusions of his lifetime of analytical thinking together with his memories and experiences, and then analyzes the resulting fabric in light of his professional training and experience as a psychiatrist and psychoanalyst.

This book also represents a memorial to Peter and is a testimony to and a description of his professional care for his patients and his lifelong research in psychiatry and psychoanalysis (especially schizophrenia and childhood autism). A most important aspect of Peter's life is that his battle with one gravely serious childhood disease after another became an overwhelming impetus for him to devote his life to medical research and the care of the mentally ill.

Simone asked me to do some editing of the book to help prepare it for publication. As I am not a medical professional and certainly not trained in the areas of psychiatry, my editing of his professional ideas and his references to a great many published works in the medical field has had to be minimal. There may be some errors or omissions in the book. I have taken the liberty of smoothing out some of the language and altering the order of presentation where I thought this might help the reader. But, throughout, I have attempted to capture the spirit of Peter's materials.

As Peter's "little brother," I have always recognized his powerful intellect, his superhuman drive, love of fun and his wide range of interests. When he was about twelve years old and had read through and "digested" Shakespeare's *Hamlet – Prince of Denmark*, he rewrote it, he simplified the text and he presented his production to the hotel guests (for fifteen cents a seat) in the ballroom of our Aunt Kate Cornell's hotel on the south side of Chicago, the Hyde Park Hotel. Peter was the producer, the director, the set designer, the stage manager, the box-office manager, the promoter, the chief usher … and, of course, Peter was Hamlet, the Prince of Denmark.

His cast of six or seven little kids, including me as (an eight year old) Polonius, were all a delight, I'm told, and Peter's production was a smashing success for all the audience. Was this, perhaps, Peter's very first claim to fame?

*Tom King*
*March 20, 2002*

# PREFACE

## BY MARK FISHER, M.D.

*Reader's Digest* used to have a monthly article about the most unforgettable person ever met. For me, Peter King was the one. Peter was a brilliant man, a psychiatrist and psychoanalyst (teacher and practitioner), a remarkably innovative thinker and philosopher, a superb athlete, a wonderful parent for his children and a profound parent-figure for his patients.

I knew Peter during the last 25 years of his life. He had an enormous influence on me, and what he taught, implicitly and explicitly, was that there really aren't any limits to the scope of human accomplishment. Trained as a Freudian psychoanalyst, his message was compatible with the human potentials movement, with its emphasis on self-actualization, and included a subtle and gracious spirituality, which Jung would have understood very well. He lived and taught the mind-body relationship by exercising, always exercising, the mind (brutally honest self-examination) and body (marathons, triathlons, *et al.*). I have become utterly convinced that in terms of a concise life-message and instructions for self-fulfillment, it doesn't get any better than this.

I hope that readers will get a sense of the scope of the man, the range of his interests, and the fascinating and important ideas he shares with us all. Was Peter King a genius? That's a question to be left to the reader. I reached my own answer to that one some time ago. What cannot be contested was Peter's capacity to empower others to listen for, and maybe even hear, a kind of genius within.

*Mark Fisher, M.D.*
*Irvine, California*
*April 2002*

Mark Fisher is Professor of Neurology at the University of California at Irvine.

# FOREWORD
## NOTES FROM THE COUCH*
## BY RIA PARODY ERLICH

Peter King was the second therapist I called from the list of three given to me by a local referral service when I was living in the San Fernando Valley, more specifically in Van Nuys, California. I was immediately drawn to him from our first phone conversation because he was willing to accommodate my schedule and find time to see me, unlike the first shrink I called who self-importantly made certain I knew how busy he was and that he would be doing me a gargantuan favor to squeeze me in. In addition, the first shrink told me he would be unable to see me in his San Fernando Valley office, but would only be able to see me at his second place in – was it Pasadena? Peter's only office was conveniently located in Encino, relatively close to where I lived.

The deal was sealed near the end of my first meeting with Peter when I finally stopped to catch my breath after telling him non-stop for almost an hour my entire life history, including about how I had a difficult relationship with my father, but really – no, REALLY – loved my mother, and what I

---

\*   There was a couch in Peter's office, but it was of the living room sofa variety and not the stereotypical psychiatrist's "divan," as seen in cartoons, movies, etc. I did not lie down on it but, rather, sat on it for a few sessions until I realized that I was more comfortable talking with him while sitting in the chair next to his desk. Thus, this piece should be called, more literally and less metaphorically, "Notes from the Chair Next to the Desk."

wanted from therapy. At that point, Peter asked me, "What's going on?" To my amazement and delight, he had detected, without my having said a word about it, that my mind was not fully on my session, but partly on something else. In fact, immediately prior to my appointment with Peter, I had been involved in a difficult meeting with some members of a community theater group to which I belonged at the time, and had left feeling angry, frustrated and humiliated. I was still feeling that way, but hadn't even brought it up! I knew then and there that this man, who seemed acutely attuned and sensitive to my moods and thoughts, was the shrink for me!

Due to financial constraints, I started seeing Peter every other week, then weekly, when I had a few more dollars in my pockets. After a year or so, Peter invited me to join one of his therapy groups, and I accepted. So, ultimately, I saw him twice a week, once in my "individual" session and once in "group," for two decades, ending with his death in the year 2000.

People relate to their therapists differently, seeing them as parents, siblings, teachers, mentors, etc. In my case, I saw Peter as a "pal," though it took me several years to feel comfortable enough to stop calling him "Dr. King" and use his first name. He did not take nor refer to notes during my sessions, but gave me his undivided attention and remarkably remembered all the details of my life, week to week and year to year. He was, for me, a non-critical, non-judgmental friend, who knew and accepted me completely and unconditionally.

Even though for the most part I talked and he listened, Peter was an active participant in my sessions, which I thoroughly appreciated and enjoyed (a shrink who only listens, nods and utters an occasional 'uh huh' or 'hmmm…' is definitely not my type). And he was not shy about offering insights and opinions to help me grow and mature. Nothing was off limits for discussion, because Peter strongly believed that "whatever comes up comes up for a reason," and that, no matter how mundane, everything is relevant in therapy and could often lead to something else that was deeper and more profound. As a result, I felt free to talk with him about any subject at all, down to the minutiae of daily living. He, in turn, would share anecdotes about his family and proffer theories on everything from where to get the best prices on electronics equipment and which running shoes to buy to investing in financial markets and real estate. He also did not hesitate to ask for and was genuinely interested in – my advice on a variety of topics, which went a long way toward giving me the ego-boost I needed.

Additionally, he was the best emotional and physical role model I or anyone, in my opinion – could have. He exuded self-confidence (some, including Peter, might say to the point of sometimes seeming arrogant or a braggart), which, for someone loaded with self-doubt like me, was gratifying and refreshing. But he wouldn't hesitate to tell stories about himself to demonstrate that he was as flawed and human as everyone else. Peter certainly had definite ideas and opinions on how things ought to be done, but did not feel there was only one "right way." He truly respected my ideas, opinions and points of view (and I could be every bit as adamant and passionate when discussing mine as he could be when discussing his), even when we differed. He believed that change was possible for everyone, including him, and discouraged use of words like "always" and "never."

Peter also spoke proudly of his athletic prowess, which was considerable, and encouraged his patients to take care of their bodies as well as their minds. It is because of him that today, at age 55, I jog, lift free weights and do stomach crunches regularly, as well as play golf and tennis and ride my bicycle as often as possible.

Clearly, though Peter died two years ago, I still feel his influence and presence daily. Only recently have I begun to stop saying, "Peter SAYS," and started more often to say, "Peter USED to say." He touched my life profoundly in many ways for many years and continues to do so. I, like so many others, feel exceptionally lucky to have known and loved him.

Peter, I'll – sorry – ALWAYS remember and NEVER forget you.

*Ria Parody Erlich August 2002*

# ACKNOWLEDGMENTS

First and foremost I offer my thanks to my brother-in-law, Tom King, for his extensive initial editing of my husband's original manuscript and to Ria Parody Erlich and my daughter, Ariela Rubin (née Clara Young Kim), for their important editing of the final text. I also thank my son, Johannes J. Kim, for his expert computer assistance and my daughter, Carol D. King, for her loving, emotional support throughout this project.

I would also like to acknowledge and thank my family, friends, colleagues and Dr. Peter King's patients, whom I am grateful and honored to know. Special thanks to the following people who gave me an advice for a means of life and an encouragement on the publication of the book: Dr. and Mrs. Mark Fisher; Mr. Arnold and Mrs. Blanch Belnick; Mr. Tibor and Mrs. Ardath Zelig; Mr. Don Warfield; Mr. and Mrs. Chris Wangsgard; Mr. and Mrs. John Cornell; Ms. Alison Cornell; Mr. Edward and Mrs. Mona Foulke; Dr. Barry Panter; Dr. Sidney Russak; Dr. Marcia Goin; Dr. Judd Marmor; Dr. and Mrs. Peter Loewenberg; Dr. Marvin and Mrs. Pat Osman; Dr. Kenneth House; Dr. and Mrs. John Peck; Dr. and Mrs. Tom Willson; Drs. Lawrence and Kato Pomer; Dr. and Mrs. Norman Levy; Dr. Albert Schrut and Mrs. Sherry Schrut; Dr. Mary Thompsen; Dr. Carlo DeAntonio and Mrs. Madeline DeAntonio; Dr. John A. Lindon; Dr. Hindy Nobler; Dr. and Mrs. Robert Caraway; Dr. and Mrs. Jose Amador; Dr. and Mrs. Alfred Coodley; Dr. and Mrs. Erwin Shirtz; Drs. Telfer Reynolds; Dr. and Mrs.

John Leonard; Dr. Sumner Shapiro; Dr. Edwin Kleinmen; Dr. and Mrs. Terrence Taylor; Dr. Raj Sethi; Dr. B. Kordan; Mr. Jeffrey A. Murad; Ms. Shayne Carter; Ms. Loura Eve Goldstin; Ms. Nina Rubinstein; Ms. Beanca Reis; Bernard Schulhof, Esq. and Mrs. Martha Schulhof; Mr. Barry and Mrs. Fay Herzog; Mr. Bruce Moore; Dayle Bailey, Esq.; Dr. Althea J. Homer; Chris Morton, Esq.; Mr. Thomas A. Norton; Ms. Anne C. Batten; Ms. Lourdes M. King; Ms. Leslie Rudin; Ms. Robin Prudhomme; Mr. Bruce B Moore; Mrs. Marcia Rosenthal; Ms. Donna Duran; Mrs. Kathleen Vanderburgh; Ms. Catherine Carter; Ms. Lilian Fleiderman; Mr. and Mrs. Harry Payne; Ms. Karen L. Emerson; I am also very grateful for the terrific support of: Joshua, Ariela (née Clara), David, Oshrat, and Avichayil Rubin; Johannes, Tracy, Alexander Kim and Audrey; Carol King; Yang Sup, Jin Young, Grace, and Edward Cho; Mr. Robert and Dr. Sophia Pak; Mr. Chris and Mrs. Jenny Pfaff; Mr. Mike and Mrs. Pat Moore; Ms. Michiko Karubi; Everette Meiners, Esq. and Mrs. Carole Meiners; Ms. Jennifer Meiners; Ms. Hillary Meiners; Mr. and Mrs. Tyler Little; Ms. Shirley Pontious; Mr. and Mrs. Victor Barciki; Mrs. Jung Sook Kim; Mrs. Sung Ok Lee; Mr. and Mrs. John Van Edgemont; Mrs. Roberta Nicholson; Mr. Edward Kwinn; Mike Mears Esq. and Mrs. Susie Mears; Ms. Julia Mears; Eugene Rudolph Esq. and Mrs. Teasha Rudolph; Dr. Robert Romer; Dr. William Tucker and Mrs. Deborah Romer-Tucker; Dr. Blair and Mrs. Christine Romer; Daniel Robyn, Esq. and Cheril Romer-Robyn, Esq.; Dr. Robert Warmmington and Mrs. Joan Warmmington; Mr. Lyle Harper Jr; Mr. and Mrs. John C. Kim; Dr. Michell Oh; Dr. and Mrs. Ivan Thomas; Mr. and Mrs. William Yang; Mr. and Mrs. Bob Thomas; Mr. and Mrs. Milton Gray; Mr. and Mrs. Mark Bae; Ms. Jee Young Chung; Mrs. Agnes Song; Ms. Sue Chung; Mr. Al and Mrs. Jean Stoffels; Mr. and Mrs. Glen Blair; Peter Double, Esq. and Mrs. Soojin Double; Mr. and Mrs. Leonard Brown; Ms. Yeong Y, Suh; Mrs. Romie Haden; Mr. and Mrs. Dudley Lee; Drs. Ron and Sunny Melendez; Mr. and Mrs. Roger Bullock; Mr. Al and Mrs. Tuim Wever; Ms. June

Bentulan; Mrs. Aileen Park; Mrs. Audrey Zacharias; Mr. Larry Jr. Zacharias; Ms. Lisa Zacharias; Drs. Hai Ahn and Hazel Kim; Mrs. Celia Gerry; Mrs. Reeta Karmarkar; Mrs. Angelika Wilkinson; Mrs. Ruth Altenbach; Mrs. Analies Stahnke; Mrs. Sevil Ben Li; Ms. Heide Marie; Mr. and Mrs. Timothy Mulholland; Lynette Kim, Esq.; Mrs. Sun Ja Kim; Mr. Mark Fredric and Mrs. Gaylan Fredric; Dr. Russ and Mrs. Julie Coser; Tim O'crowley, Esq. and Mrs. Sarah O'crowley; Mr. and Mrs. Blaine Webber; Mr. and Mrs. Dwight Hikkila; Mr. and Mrs. Bob Mullen; Mr. and Mrs. Neil Farren; Dr. Lester and Mi Ja Goldsmith; Mrs. Harry Easton; Mrs. Chung Sook Miller; Mr. and Mrs. Thomas Sail; Mr. Peter Sail; Mrs. Elizabeth Davis; Mrs. Phyllis Belcher; Mrs. Patricia Burdette; Dr. Sun Hai Choi; Ms. Kookhwa Lee; Mrs. Sinok Wolf; Ms. Fran Raming; Mr. and Mrs. Erne Carpenter; Dr. and Mrs. Michael H Wenning; Rev. Carolyn Crawford; Ms. Trudy McCulley; Ms. Criss Rowan; Mrs. Jan Kolstad; Mrs. Mary Lou Reid; Mr. John Petti; Ms. Carol Daniel; Ms. Mary Erickson; Ms. Barbara Vigi; Ms. Carolyn Simonds; Stephen Tayler, Esq. and Kathryn Tayler, Esq; Ms. Jean Siegel; Ms. Virginia Gregory; Mrs. Cindy Copmton; Mrs. Carol Moomaw; Mrs. Alice Carpenter; Mrs. Barbara Hoche; Ms. Victoria Iskowitz; Mrs. Margaret Thompson; Ms. Frances Davidson; Mrs. Beverly Kerr; and Mrs. Elise Haig; Mrs. Bettye Woodworth; Ms. Norma Krueger; Mrs. Anna Kerr; Mrs. Peggy Barbour; Mrs. Marion Martin; Mrs. Maxine Burns; Mrs. Loraine Mcdougale.

*Simone M. King*

# PREFACE
## BY PETER D. KING, M.D., PH.D.

Life is fleeting and time is relative, yet the pace of our lives seems only to accelerate. Once it took several months to travel across our vast country by horse and wagon. Now we jet from coast to coast in just a few hours. As our media of communication give us information in a few seconds and we respond in similar fashion by telephone, cell phone, fax and e-mail, we begin to lose our roots, our history and our skills. Increasing numbers of us are hardly able to read, write or even speak our language very well and many of us are losing the ability to reckon without a calculator. Some even claim that the Holocaust never occurred. We are losing our connections with each other and our world.

Early in human history we could only use signs and gestures to communicate our feelings and ideas. We gradually advanced as we added speech, painting, song and dance – and later, recordings in books, tapes and computer disks. Now that process seems to be reversing as tapes are destroyed and disks are erased to make space for an increasing mass of trivia. Much of our artistic, intellectual and scientific heritage may fade away, while the environment deteriorates to a residue of what once existed.

Testimony to this is furnished by the compasses that shall never be used to find our way through the woods, running shoes that shall no longer be worn to run through clean air, and cries that shall never be heard by people wired into cubicles. Remnants of the past are the animals in the zoo and the fish in the aquarium that provide only a sample of what used to exist in our forests and seas and now head for extinction. Patches of redwoods, scattered tide pools and polluted beaches serve as poor reminders of what used to be. The loss of nature with which to connect is matched by the loss of our bonds with other humans as we increasingly connect by electronic devices that suck us into a mechanized world. We are losing our humanity and it appears that we are becoming too alienated or too fearful to acknowledge and even to recognize what is happening to us.

This book is – in part — a protest against this process. It is an attempt to remind us of our connections with our families, our friends and our emotions and minds. It is an autobiography in which I present my own lifetime of experience and its many connections to my world. [Note that my many annotations to the text appear in brackets [ ] and are separated from the main text.]

As I present my life story and my ideas, I ask you to stop and listen to my "voice of genius," a voice that is within us all. I ask you to hear it and speak its truth now and to feel its message to be your own message that you boldly give to others next to you and far away from you. Please read it and listen to what it says for you. Even if it is too late, there is a chance that it is not. Even if you are too young, too old or too sick to believe that you can speak your voice of genius, do it, do it now and do it over and over again.

I write this autobiography for you as well as myself. Like me, you also come from the earth, the flesh and the blood and have reached out and will continue to reach out to the people around you; and the trees, the sky and the stars. And you will wonder with me. You will recognize in it your own childhood, your own frustrations and your own triumphs. You will also recognize your need to be strong, to trust yourself, to trust others and to connect with them. But above all, you will recognize that you were, you are and you will continue to be part of the structure of our universe no matter what you do. And if you are able and willing to read, digest and apply my arguments, you will see the decency and the goodness that also dwell in your own heart and mind and can emerge from you—regardless of what is out there.

Like children, at times we are mean, temperamental and selfish with each other. But also like children, we are capable of loving each other. I write this book with my love for that part of you and that part of myself that has learned these things. In that sense, we are brothers, sisters and friends.

And *we are the voice of genius*.

*Peter D. King, M.D., Ph.D.*

# CHAPTER I

## INTRODUCTION

I slowly gain consciousness in a dark, bleak room with a tube up my nose and down the back of my throat and with needles in my arms. My limbs are taped to boards that are strapped to the bed, and for an eternity I keep drifting in and out of awareness in the total absence of any other creature. I am shivering because the fluid going into my arms makes me feel extremely cold. I begin to sense pain that I can no longer ignore. My belly is wrapped with bandages from which comes a putrid smell that is even worse than the stench of my body.

I remember being rushed to Cook County Hospital in Chicago on a Saturday afternoon in January with severe pain in my right lower abdomen, only to lie alone on a Gurney cart in an empty corridor for what must have been six to eight hours. Then, I was taken to an operating room and told by one of the masked figures to count as he or she started dripping ether on gauze on a small metal cage over my face. The ether felt cold and increasingly like hundreds of needle pricks as I began to count. A buzzing sound started to fill the remaining silence. By the time I reached six or seven, my voice seemed to echo in a peculiar way, like "siyiyiyix," "seyeveveven," "eighyayayayayt," "niyiyiyiyine." That was the last I remembered.

Until now. I am awake for a brief time and then fall back to sleep and have two dreams. In the first, my mouth is very full of teeth and,

1

as I gently bite down, the teeth suddenly fracture into dozens of pieces. I begin to panic at losing the pieces, as if I could never get them back together, when the dream switches to my feet forming into a rod that holds a wheel. The wheel is a sharp, circular blade, like the blades used to slice meat in a delicatessen, and I am flying over the edge of a dark cliff. Suddenly, I turn in the air and plunge feet-first over the cliff and into the chasm. I drop hundreds of feet like a rock, accelerating to incredible speed. With great effort I turn my feet ever so slowly to use the blade like a rudder, gradually shifting direction and accelerating back up to the edge of the cliff, and I wake up. I feel like I have just managed to escape from horrible oblivion into safety.

Later, my mother tells me that I almost died that night. I recovered from a combination of scarlet fever and a ruptured appendix, which went on to become peritonitis long before there were any antibiotics. I spent most of a week in delirium and awakened to many more weeks of ongoing intravenous feeding with suction tubes in my stomach. I was able to return home after several months and spent almost a year and a half draining pus from my abdomen. Every week I went to the surgeon who saved my life, who took a stick of silver nitrate with his forceps and pushed it into the hole in my abdomen, causing me to feel unremitting nausea. This treatment continued even after I returned to elementary school, which I had been able to attend because I wore a women's girdle to hold my protruding abdomen and wounds together so that (I was told) my insides would not spill out into my clothes.

Even when I was coming out of coma in the hospital, a few visitors came and blessed me, in the case of an Episcopal priest, or told me how brave I was, in the case of my grandmother and other relatives. Most of those visits were ordeals for me because I was so exhausted. Often the good wishes and compliments on my bravery sounded hollow to me, probably because it was no choice of mine to be there, and if I could have escaped from my predicament, I would have left immediately.

[I was skeptical of those good wishes, but I was also grateful for the sentiments — even if they were more form than substance. I respect such form. It is very important to use it and to be grateful for its use; and, as I became more mature I was able to acknowledge it more graciously. Still, at times, I can become internally impatient.

For example, when I was close to thirty and had already published my initial ideas on schizophrenia, was working on my first book, *The Principle of Truth,* had several research papers close to publication, and received requests from this country and other countries around the world for reprints of my earlier research publications, my grandfather would introduce me to other people as *"a doctor."* It was difficult for me not to feel hurt at what seemed to be his lack of understanding of all that I had accomplished. It is not easy to overcome your sense of pride and even what may be arrogance. Slowly, I have emerged from my hurt feelings and been able to respond genuinely to good wishes, which is why I said, "Thank you," to the black prisoner at Tehachapi prison who said to me, "Dr. King, you is a pimp!" I knew from his manner that he was complimenting me, and I showed him my genuine gratitude.]

However, when my mother visited, I was ecstatic. I watched and waited, eager to see her when it was time for her to come. I loved her so much, and she was so warm and comforting to me that I felt a breathless weakness that I can even feel now.

I could give great detail about my hospital experiences, but I prefer to summarize by saying that all my contact with hospitals and medicine, as well as the respect I saw and shared for the doctors, led to my desire to be a doctor myself, but not *just* a doctor. Important as each person is, saving one life at a time seems too little, and, at age thirteen, I decided to become a medical scientist who would try to discover ways of eliminating illness itself. This book gives a description of this process, the context in which those things took place and the consequences that resulted.

[The peritonitis was actually my second near-fatal illness, the first being when I was four. Having become a parent myself, I can imagine the pain my parents must have felt. It is not surprising that my mother told me that God had saved my life in order for me to play some role in world history. Obviously my mother was extremely grateful that I survived.]

As testimony to good parenting by my mother and father, I was a fairly levelheaded little boy and took what my mother said with a grain of salt. Still, I felt a responsibility to the world and began to read and think about becoming a physician.

Of course, there were interruptions. Late one summer my brother, my parents and I went camping for four nights in Wisconsin. On our way home, we saw headlines that Germany had invaded Poland. My mother had tears in her eyes as she said that the world was destined for terrible suffering for the next few years.

Although the war had started, it did not affect us much until the Japanese bombed Pearl Harbor. I was more impressed by heroics than by danger, and by the time I was 16, had developed the ambition to become a hot fighter pilot. I had visited my grandfather's home in Fort Lauderdale, Florida, twice and seen the Grumman F3F2's peel out of formation among thunderheads near thirty thousand feet, spiral down toward the sea and then zoom back up into the sky.

I wanted to be a naval air force pilot for many reasons, one of which was the challenge of landing and taking off from an aircraft carrier. However, I welcomed any chance to fly, so, when I was 17 years old and the Army Air Corps offered me a free plane ride if I enlisted to become an Air Cadet, I did not hesitate to sign up, which, luckily permitted me to remain in high school for another ten months. In addition to my high-school classes, I tried to read many of the classics and near-classics of fiction and non-fiction. Among my readings were most of the writings of Freud. Although my primary ambition was to engage in cancer research, I also made the decision that I would undergo psychoanalysis.

I was called to active duty in the Army Air Forces when the war was almost over. After two years on active duty, I returned to civilian life, applied to The University of Chicago and was accepted on the basis of my mostly 99+ percentile G.E.D. tests. I completed college and pre-medical training and, ironically, attended medical school where I had been hospitalized for severe poliomyelitis. Eight years earlier, I had spent almost three months at The University of Chicago Hospitals in the Home for Destitute Crippled Children.

When I finished medical school, I had done almost everything in medicine — delivered babies; performed many surgeries, such as hernia repairs, gall bladder removal, and appendectomies; participated in some other extremely complex surgeries; taken over for the neurology intern for the few weeks he was sick; and engaged in research while working on the side 25 to 50 hours a week to help support my beginning family. I established a coagulation research laboratory at The University of Chicago Clinics and published two papers on the mechanics of blood coagulation (Spurling and King, 1954).

After many new and rich experiences in medical school, there seemed to be little mystery left for me except for psychiatry. I had read everything required for psychiatry, plus all of the recommended readings, but was especially fascinated by the patients. The psychiatry ward, which was on the third floor of Billings Hospital, held a mystique for all the medical students. What went on in there? What made those people behave so weirdly? And what made people develop schizophrenia?

*One quarter of all hospital beds in the United States in the 1950s were occupied by schizophrenic patients.*

[Among schizophrenics who spent four years or more in a state mental hospital, the probability of being released from the hospital within the following year was less than 1.60% (Kramer, M., *et al.*, 1955). To me, the complexity of the human mind, the heterogeneity of human behavior and the puzzle of schizophrenia were on the frontier where I wanted to be.]

As a medical student, I had examined schizophrenic patients at a veterans' hospital in Chicago and had an inner feeling that I could understand this disease. Discovering that I could support my family, learn psychiatry, bring statistical methods and careful research design to medicine, and work on the mystery of schizophrenia, I became a resident in psychiatry at Warren State Hospital in western Pennsylvania, a 3400-bed psychiatric hospital where 1700 men and women had schizophrenia.

I threw myself into learning psychiatry and into my research, and, in about one year, formulated the hypnosis theory of schizophrenia. All of the symptoms of schizophrenia could be duplicated in normal subjects under hypnosis, except for the most basic impairment of "associations" in which the clarity of thinking is muddled. I used normal subjects, put them into a trance and gave them the thinking tests we did everyday in testing for schizophrenia. Under hypnosis they were like schizophrenics; when they were not under hypnosis, they were not.

By hypnotizing normal people, I caused them to have the most basic disturbances of schizophrenia, contrary to the earlier ideas of Eugene Bleuler (Bleuler, E., 1950). *Bleuler had written that those basic disturbances of associations in schizophrenics had to be organic, not psychological, in origin, yet I had produced them psychologically.*

[Even Freud wrote that schizophrenia was organic in origin.]

I was excited and afraid that my ideas were so obvious to everyone that they would be published at any moment. On the one hand, I prepared my first research results for publication. But on the other hand, I wanted to begin life-long studies of mothers and their infants to try to select which ones would eventually become schizophrenic and then to follow them over the years. Once the crucial factors were recognized, pediatric teams could observe mother-infant dyads, and those who showed easily recognized cues for bonding dissonance would be selected out for intensive work with both mother and infant to try to prevent the illness. The task was economically feasible, because I believed that less than two percent of the population would need special, extra attention. However, I knew that it might well require another fifty years for me to accomplish this research. So, I became very careful about my health and tried to learn what steps I could take to live long enough to do it.

The preparation for a journey of discovery actually started when I was a little child, but the second usually fatal illness and my mother's friendship with me when I was a little boy recovering from peritonitis set me on my course. It was difficult for me as a nine-year-old agnostic to believe in God, much less that he had actually spared my life for some important role in the world, especially because my mother wanted to be a very important person herself. She often told me that some day she would be recognized as one of the world's great painters. She had received notoriety for some of her paintings shown at the Art Institute of Chicago. She priced most of her larger paintings at approximately $5,000 each and, not surprisingly in those depression years, was unable to sell any of them.

[I was a serious child who thought of many things, but never carefully organized them until adolescence. I had a natural skepticism about religion. When I was about eight years old my doubts about God and Jesus led me to fear that God was reading my mind and would punish me for my thoughts. Later I remembered that I was actually using those thoughts as an active method of testing God's existence. Because nothing happened, at least I knew that God was not punitive, unless there was some record of "black marks" being kept to give me an ultimate punishment. However, I felt as if God had to be like a kind parent, if he actually existed. Later, I decided that a punitive God was not as kind as I was and was not *worthy* of my respect.

Eventually, as I matured, I came to feel that any God who had created the world deserves compassion. Many people have denied God's existence because of the imperfections and suffering in the world. "How could God permit such suffering?" they ask.

However, God would have to be wise and either omnipotent or close to it. Perhaps any attempt to improve on the world could turn out to be a disaster. Realizing this, God might have chosen to let well enough alone.

Somehow I felt a kinship with God, like God's spirit was inside me. It was a *good* spirit, but also a lonely spirit for which I felt tears. The doubts I exercised disclosed the developing scientist in me, which began to develop rapidly. I started a habit of keeping records on a variety of things, like the survival rates of my toy soldiers in battles when I shelled them with tennis balls.]

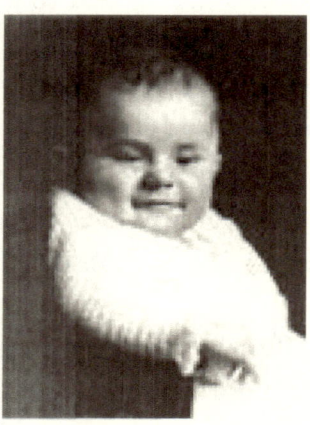

My mother told me that I weighed 7½ pounds at birth and was born one month early, but as an adolescent I thought 7½ pounds at eight months was not likely. I decided that my mother must have conceived me before her marriage and her early pregnancy was an embarrassment to her. Perhaps to balance out her embarrassment, she had developed the idea that I had a role to play in the world, especially after my third near-fatal illness at the age of fifteen.

I really loved and appreciated my mother, and some years later I also realized that she was as wonderful a parent and mother as anyone could have been. She was bright, a creative artist and, in her early twenties, wrote for two national magazines. She was very beautiful and had a forceful personality (reminding me today of a younger edition of Mia Hamm of the U.S. Women's soccer team, who won the 1999 world championship game against China).

As a child I was also very bright, with an active mind capable of playing around easily with my perceptions and thoughts. I almost never napped after the age of eighteen months, often being awake and mentally and physically active from about six-thirty every morning and seldom fell asleep until after 9 p.m.

Many times I summarized experiential things to myself. For example, in the summer when I was six, I thought to myself, "My how time goes faster as I get older. Imagine how fast it will seem when I am ten, or twenty!" More thoughts occurred along with some feeling of loss at the passage of time. I also sensed that time would be just as important to me at twenty — or whatever age I attained — as it was to me at age six.

I had a good memory, and my thoughts became a part of my being. My mother told me that at age twenty-two months I could recite twenty-two nursery rhymes, which did not seem to me at the time to be much of an accomplishment.

[I have always been blessed with good eidetic imagery. My experiences become part of me in feeling, proprioception, sight, smell, sound, taste, and touch, and in a general incorporative sense. This was illustrated by accident with one of my psychotherapy patients, whom I had not seen for several years. When she returned to Southern California and I went to greet her in my waiting room, I treated her as if I'd seen her the day before. Her feelings were badly hurt, but as we explored it, I saw that *she had been with me — inside myself — as a part of my very being.* This way of reacting allows me to "be" my patients.

I am also able to "be" where certain inanimate objects are, so I am able to find things quickly. For example, my wife Simone asked me where one of her calculators could be. Having seen it several days before in a spot on one of her tables, I went right to that spot and brought it to her. Simone would say, "Peter – you have photographic mind!"

After my mother died, I found among her belongings my elementary school report cards. Poring over them, I saw that my grades were generally only slightly above average. Although I rarely did any homework and was absent from school so often because of prolonged periods of illness, in the seventh grade I tested above twelfth grade level in my fund of general knowledge. I was really surprised by this because I tended to think that my real strength lay not in my knowledge of facts, but in my sense of fairness – my ability to assess right and wrong — and my natural ability to visualize the "big picture," the "reality" of my surroundings.]

Later, while I was in medical school, there was not enough time to study my texts and notes as much as I wished. I had to work at an outside job 25 to 50 hours a week and could sleep no more than six hours a night. I was ecstatic whenever I had the rare chance to read without interruption. I always sat in the front row of my medical school classes, so I could hear every word spoken in the lectures. I could only spare the time to read *once* through my texts and notes, so I took only a few spare lines of notes in class, listening, digesting and then writing briefly in my own words what had been said. Some of the other students in the front row seats took pages and pages of notes and then failed to pass the course. I could learn quickly, but being forced to take digested, meaningful notes in class permitted me to learn more effectively.

I felt a great responsibility to learn everything offered me in medical school and to become a top-notch doctor. The "medical world" had saved my life so very often, and I had the responsibility to repay my great debt to it.

[I have always been noted for my abundant energy and drive. Some psychiatric colleagues have even claimed that I am *hypomanic*! Is this true? Once I began taking 300 milligrams of lithium carbonate every night to see if there was any change in my behavioral mood. There was no effect! I stopped for a while and then tried again for another ten days just to be sure, but there was still no change. Several times I skipped sleep entirely and cut out eating any food, but I was still fully able to study, to work, and to be social and almost fully alert. Those are just two examples of how I have used myself as an experimental subject.]

After completing my medical school training at The University of

Chicago, I began to explore many of my early beliefs more methodically and began applying my accumulated knowledge towards some medical discoveries.

This book presents my ideas as they pop into my consciousness, rather than in some topically organized order. Some of my ideas are unique. Only some have been published. The validity of some of my ideas may be questioned. Regardless, I feel a responsibility to present all of them to you here, along with the pertinent background information.

# CHAPTER II
# PROFESSIONAL IDEAS
# AND MUSINGS

## SCHIZOPHRENIA

I am the author of the "hypnosis theory" of schizophrenia, which I formulated in 1955, tested the evidence for in 1956, and which was finally published (King, 1957). In brief, the paper said that symptom formation in schizophrenia, regardless of any "organic" or genetic factors, occurs through hypnosis from within the personality. As people age and face the threats of relationships, school, exploding sexual desire, work, career, marriage and leaving home, those who become schizophrenic utilize patterns of behavior they have already developed in their earliest infancy. They escape from those threats by becoming detached and entering a state of "trance." The "primary symptom," the classical schizophrenic difficulty in concentrating (the "disturbance of associations," per Bleuler, 1950), is the result of the trance itself, while the "secondary" symptoms of delusions, hallucinations and others are the result of "hypnotic" suggestion from inner wishes, fears and other emotions that act from the conscious and inner, unconscious mind.

[I am talking about behavior that is automatic and beyond control, direction or cognitive awareness (akin to the worm that turns away automatically from heat or other threats to its comfort and survival). As humans mature, including schizophrenics, they usually develop an awareness of the reasons for their behavior even though they may be unable to control it.]

In a later paper (King, 1965), I pointed out that some of the seeming oppositional symptoms in schizophrenia represent the return of "bonding dissonance" — a transferential punishment of the environment today for the experiences of infancy and childhood. I originally referred to this as "the return of the double bind." Not only will these symptoms drive others away, they will also punish the world today for the pain experienced yesterday.

[This set of phenomena in schizophrenia acquires special significance in light of the evidence that an early "bonding dissonance" is crucial to the eventual development of the disease. These phenomena, besides arising from the splitting of consciousness, express (in an automatic way) the psychological need to repeat, mock, or avoid a would-be "double bind" interaction and are a regressive repetition of the presumed early "double bind" relationship. They include affect disturbances, certain disturbances of speech and writing, ambivalence, stereotypes, automatisms, command automatisms, negativism and waxy flexibility. Some of these can be seen as distorted, restitutive attempts to communicate, at the same time serving to undo or minimize the implication of what is being communicated. By using them, "the schizophrenic dramatizes earlier attempts to break through the 'double bind'," which discouraged straightforward communication. Their function is like that of the court jester who could express criticism of the monarch only if what he said was couched in a jest accompanied by foolish behavior, which diverted attention from the deeper meaning of the jest.]

Thus patients may show an absence, exaggeration or displacement in speech — they may speak loudly, softly, rapidly or slowly, or may make peculiar gestures or scribblings. They may speak in a falsetto, mumble or grunt, make strange body movements or decorate themselves in bizarre fashion. The patient who smiles sweetly as she whispers obscenities tries with her affect and her voice to undo the hostility she expresses. Other of these phenomena have a mocking quality — thus in command automatism and waxy flexibility the patient presents a caricature of conformity.

[As the psychoanalyst Otto Fenichel pointed out, everyone – even the most regressed, catatonic schizophrenic – has the impulse to connect with other people. Among schizophrenics, such attempts can be pitifully feeble or almost invisible, drive others away and manifest themselves in many ways. Fenichel called these attempts, which even include hallucinations, "restitutive symptoms" (Fenichel, 1945).]

Imagine the catatonic patients whose limbs may be raised by others and remain in the position where they are left in for hours at a time. It is like they are demonstrating to the world that they are in total conformity with the "totalitarians" surrounding them, saying with their body language, "Look at what a total piece of clay I must be to survive with these people." This "mockery" often infuriates those around them, which is probably part of its inner purpose (and reminds me of Till Owlglass [Eulenspiegel], who played pranks on other people and repeatedly made mistakes in his seemingly conscientious attempts to help his mother and run errands for her). Of course, this behavior has many determinants, but the fact that it is so pronounced is consistent with the HTS (hypnosis theory of schizophrenia) and is further evidence that "bonding dissonance" is crucial to the development of schizophrenia.

In recent years psychiatry has offered the concept of "negative" symptoms in which reduced facial expression, poor eye contact, reduced body language, poverty of speech and an absence of motivation are observed (American Psychiatric Association, 1994). It is not difficult to see how such behavior may serve to keep others at a distance.

[I once wrote a poem titled "Jesster" (my use of the double "s" is deliberate) that portrays some of the interpersonal transactions that occur among schizophrenic people as they become adults (King, 1996). It was a poetic expression of the idea that families of schizophrenic people can sometimes impose a weird heritage (such as a strange name) that may even help to *cause* the child to be out of step with the world. The quotations in the poem represent massive denial by the family (and other people in Jesster's immediate world) that they see anything disparaging in Jesster's behavior. It is too unpleasant to acknowledge the idea that they could in any way have been *responsible* for Jesster's behavior, even though they may be totally innocent of causing a condition that is genetic in origin. This is especially true because Jesster has mocked and blamed them over and over again for causing the bonding dissonance that he discovered when he was born into the world.

## JESSTER

He smiles and smiles, the Jester smiles,
And bows and scrapes "How nice he is!"
He smiles, and as he smiles,
"No voices in his head entice and tease."
He smiles, and as he smiles,
"He thinks no vile obscenities!"
He smiles, the Jester smiles,
And in his heart "No bitter price it is."
"Those smiles aren't wiles," the Jester's smiles
"Do not reveal" what inner ice it is
That froze the Jester's smile
Long, long ago. ]

Any psychiatrists or others in the past who in any way blamed parents for the schizophrenia in their children were not really scientific. They had jumped to a conclusion that was not necessarily correct, perhaps led by the implicit criticism of parents in the propaganda repeatedly dispensed by "Jesster" and others who are like him. At the other extreme, those who claimed that schizophrenia is entirely genetic in origin were also unscientific in their neglect of interactive factors in the development of symptom patterns in this disease.

Much later, I read that in 1960, R. D. Laing had touched on my ideas when he said that schizophrenia was not an illness, but a method of adaptation. (By the way — I believe now that *all illnesses are, to a major extent, methods of adaptation.*) Laing also said that many schizophrenic symptoms serve to mock those people around them (Laing, 1969) — in what I later called the return of the "double bind." Although my ideas were formulated well before I knew of Laing, his ideas about mockery preceded mine. However, like other researchers, he did not see the origins to be in the earliest mother- infant dyad, much less as the result of the infant's withdrawal from "bonding dissonance" (or words to that effect). Instead he saw the origins of schizophrenia and of the mockery accompanying it to be after the first year of life, or even in "childhood," as a result of the influence of the "father or other significant adults."

Here are my ideas on this.

During the formation of the ego in the first seven months of life, some infants withdraw into a primitive trance. This establishes a fixed pathway that can be used later to escape from stress by those becoming schizophrenic. Delusions, hallucinations and other schizophrenic symptoms are the result of hypnosis from inner wishes, conflicts and fears. In *The Divided Self*, Laing discusses several cases, including "Julie," at the end of the book. The clinical documentation of the "ego splits" in "Julie" and other cases is similar to many authors who discuss such issues. To me, these issues are virtually infinite and emerge directly from the hypnotic detachment in the first months of life and from all of the later experiences of loneliness, isolation and the wide range of family interactions experienced by the designated patient, which, together, created an infinite variety of behavior.

Some of these ideas are conveyed in my 1957 paper, "Hypnosis and Schizophrenia," while in the paper "Ego Development and the Hypnosis Theory of Schizophrenia," (King, 1970) I said that "bonding dissonance" (which I then referred to as the "double bind") has "other effects on the developing child. We can see that it and other factors too may well result in deep feelings of insecurity, unimportance, and loneliness so common among schizophrenics, in addition to all of the other needs, fears, and conflicts which people acquire in growing up...." In addition, other psychological forces pushed from within the conscious and unconscious mind to the pre- schizophrenic individual and, "depending upon their strength, pattern, and the vicissitudes of current circumstances and relationships with others...," affected the ego to yield changes in its "perception, integration, and interpretation of reality." In other words, every schizophrenic person has a unique pattern of conflicts, which causes each case of schizophrenia to be unique, regardless of the fact that the core pathogenesis of this disease is similar for all.

*Although family interactions and the details of how they affect symptom formation are extremely important in the specific patterns of each individual case, they are almost infinite in their variety and they are independent of my core idea of what schizophrenia is and how it develops.*

## THE PRINCIPLE OF TRUTH

I developed my early philosophical views back in 1954, when I was in my late twenties. My ideas became the basis for my book, *The Principle of Truth* (King, 1960). My book starts out by agreeing with Descartes' famous view that one cannot be certain of anything except "I think, therefore I am." Even if there is nothing else in the universe, the fact that I exist is sufficient to establish reality and to establish the value of perceiving, understanding, appreciating and even loving that reality. From my point of view, the fact that I exist is sufficient *in itself* to give meaning and value to our lives; God and his moral laws are not needed.

My view on this seems to me to be more efficient than attempting to justify morality and reality by dogma, including the contortions of Talmudic law and Christianity, the complex stratifications of Hinduism, the denials and suffering of Buddhism and the frequent brutalities of Muhammadanism. Descartes (and then Kant) went further than necessary in their dependence on God's existence to establish the foundations of their beliefs.

Plato presented the pursuit of truth almost as an *a priori* principle of behavior, even though he made reference to God as its source. Descartes experientially demonstrated the existence of truth and reality with his "I think, therefore I am," but then backed off by bringing God into the picture anyway. Nietzsche finally took the step of discarding God, but ignored morality and became preoccupied with the "superman," perhaps because he felt incredibly daring at his rejection of God. My acceptance of Descartes and my enlargement on his theories to establish a stronger reality — even if it only consisted of me — was a major step, in my opinion, which led to an important, but partial, establishment of morality. In this book, I give a stronger rationale for morality.

The idea that there can be morality and reality without the need for God is valid, because the *possibility* that they exist *on their own* is always present. Even the possibility that there is a God and that there is immortality is always present. Each of these possibilities is sufficient grounds in itself to establish the presence of morality and reality. "Behave as if your behavior were a standard for a perfect universe," to modify Kant's "categorical imperative," because there just might be a perfect universe, and what a tragedy to ignore it simply because we are not sure about it. Perhaps a name for this point of view would be the "Philosophy of Possibility."

Living according to this point of view engages in morality and implies the existence of reality. Regardless of how fleeting it may be, its history is part of the fabric of space and time.

[This idea could be used to accept and practice all of the various aspects of any religion with the rationale that they could *possibly* be true. Is there a way we can reject religions insofar as they judge people too harshly and/or call for excessively complicated rituals of behavior affecting our work, play and financial well-being? The idea needs to be addressed in some detail in order to clarify these issues beyond simply pointing out their improbability and by taking into account the gradient in religion between the more primitive authoritarian aspects and the more advanced humanitarian aspects, as discussed by Albert Einstein (1952) and Erich Fromm (1970).]

A wonderful book on the current state of science — which also addresses the issues of religion and God — is *The Whole Shebang* by

Timothy Ferris. I feel that my book, *The Principle of Truth,* approaches the same ideas he expressed in his last chapter where he writes,

> One can learn to live with ambiguity ... and with the silence of the stars. All who genuinely seek to learn, whether atheist or believer, scientist or mystic, are united in having not *a* faith but faith itself. Its token is reverence, its habit to respect the eloquence of silence. For God's hand may be a human hand, if you reach out in loving kindness, and God's voice your voice, if you but speak the truth (Ferris, 1998).

[I do not wish to convey any personal belief in God by quoting Ferris but only to point out that the process of seeking and communicating truth has a unique quality of goodness, morality and even nobility. The religious air inherent in this process is testimony to my idea that such thoughts are a root from which most of the great religions emerged.]

## COSMON, ANTI-COSMON, AND PARITY IN THE UNIVERSE

A lack of "parity" was reported regarding our universe (Yang and Lee, 1956; Goldhaber, 1956; Peaslee, 1956; and Rodberg and Weisskopf, 1957), with elements showing an imbalance in clockwise versus counterclockwise rotations. Although it occurred at minor levels of energy, it did appear that the universe was "out of balance." In reaction to this finding, I pointed out that negative does not exist in our universe except in mathematical representation (King, 1957, 1960) and suggested that an "anti-cosmon," where "$i$" was "plus one," could and perhaps did exist in reality and could re-establish parity.

In 1997, I discussed this further (King, 1997) and thought that this approach could apply to Heisenberg's uncertainty principle. In essence, at least one other universe exists, especially the "anti- cosmon," which I had proposed in 1957 and said may exist anywhere in relation to "our" universe. Insofar as "spin" balanced out between the cosmon and anti-cosmon, the position of the two relative to each other might be irrelevant, and the point of origin (if any) of our universe could be anywhere in space and time. Issues of the "symmetry" and the age of the universe would be connected with its origins from zero time-space windows of transition between the cosmon and anti-cosmon and between wave behavior and particle behavior. The "pulse" and "wave" natures of matter would emerge by the passage of matter between one universe and the other, perhaps in a "big bang" (like a heavy police officer breaking through an apartment door). A digital "pulse" in matter would be required to break through the window, but once freed into another universe, would expand freely as an analog "wave," which somehow carried its "pulse" quality as a necessary companion.

Beethoven is my favorite composer and, to me, the greatest composer of all time. Regardless of Mozart's genius and music that takes us to the very edge, he has a certain complacency that holds us within our realm and our time frame. Beethoven, in a tortured process of creation, goes beyond Mozart and all of the other great composers, not only through the music itself, but by conveying an impatience that encompasses the here and now. Yet he keeps saying to us, "What is next," and, "What comes after that?" By the introduction, presentation and repetition of many musical themes, Beethoven keeps knocking on the door of the next universe like my metaphorical police officer above.

## BONDING DISSONANCE
## AND SCHIZOPHRENIA

When I read Gill and Brenman's (1961) discussion of findings on the behavior of the Balinese (Bateson, G. and Mead, M., 1942), I saw that it applied to my "hypnosis theory" of schizophrenia, which I then revised. I presented my revisions and their implications at psychoanalytic meetings in 1965, 1966 and 1967. Some of my ideas were never published; others were not published until 1970 (King, 1970).

I said that schizophrenic symptoms originated in the mother-infant dyad between three and seven months of age. Not in childhood, but in earliest infancy, a "double bind," or what I later called "bonding dissonance," occurred between mother and infant, causing the infant to detach and withdraw into a primitive kind of "trance" and to leave a pathway that could later be used under stress.

[By the way, Gregory Bateson who was the major discussant of my paper, advised me privately to ignore other research, including what had been done by his old research group in Palo Alto, California, and to go my own way.]

*"Bonding dissonance" should not be confused with rejection or deprivation,* although an infant's detachment from it might well result in deprivation. On this point, I said recently (King, 1999),

> Psychiatric patients make up 25% to 50% of our prison population, of which many are under active treatment at any one time. Some of these patients are schizophrenic, but a large proportion of them have major depression "with psychosis," psychosis secondary to substance abuse and an excess of bipolar disorder. They are different from schizophrenics, who are usually paranoid and detached, and often remain in poor personal contact, even after they overcome their psychotic symptoms. In contrast, those who are psychotic but not schizophrenic often become warm, responsive and even very close to the people they trust when they lose their psychotic symptoms. They seem to be more likely to have suffered neglect, violence and abuse in their infancy and early childhood than the "bonding dissonance" I believe to be responsible for the symptoms of schizophrenia.

[Deprivation occurs when the infant: a) remains in an incubator; b) is orphaned; c) is abandoned, beaten, left alone for hours at a time, molested, psychologically abused and/or rejected; d) is the victim of attempted murder by the active policy of a mean-spirited parent who overtly or covertly hates the infant; e) is the victim of passive treatment by a parent who is depressed, distracted by drugs or television, self-centered, sick, unconscious or unavailable for other reasons; or f) is unresponsive due to drugs or genetic heritage. In the extreme, 37% of severely deprived children may die, while the survivors may be 65% of their normal height and weight, have uncontrolled toilet habits, be unable to walk, talk, or feed themselves and have developmental quotients 65 to 75% of normal for their age (Spitz, 1965). It is no surprise that parents of schizophrenic or autistic children were horrified by the idea that they had inflicted such deprivation on their children. It was unfair and incorrect to convey that such things had occurred when these parents were probably trying their hardest to do the right thing with children, who may well have been genetically, structurally, chemically, or emotionally incapable of responding to them.]

"Bonding dissonance" can be imagined as the creepy feeling of disgust a mother would have in nursing a huge cockroach (something Franz Kafka probably sensed and conveyed in his short story *Metamorphosis*). On the one hand, a mother in such a situation would feel love for a baby she wanted, had carried in her womb and was her responsibility to care for. But on the other hand, she would also feel overwhelming disgust that the baby would perceive in a primitive, pre-cognitive way. Regardless of "organic" or other factors responsible for schizophrenia, I saw this as the mechanism by which the symptoms developed.

## BONDING DISSONANCE AND
## INFANTILE AUTISM

On November 20, 1970, I was in my office with a classically autistic boy. His mother sat in the chair beside my desk while he moved frantically around the room flapping his arms and bouncing on his toes. He touched the drapes, feeling the fabric sensuously as if it were velvet. Then he dropped to the floor and began crawling on the carpet, using his fingers to pull on the loops. His progress took him toward his mother, and I saw her pull her foot back from him, tilt her head away from him, and appear to cringe. Immediately I realized I was witnessing "bonding dissonance," which I had seen as the cause of schizophrenia. In shaking excitement that night I wrote a fairly complete description of the development of symptoms in autistic children (King, 1970, Appendix "A").

Later, I asked the mother if she had ever felt repelled by her son. She said she certainly did, having felt repelled by him from the very beginning of his infancy. She added that she had felt a similar reaction around her father. What I wrote that November 20 was supported by my later research, written in an unpublished book I circulated among almost one hundred colleagues around the country and in other parts of the world in 1973 (King, 1973). It was finally published in a short version in 1975 (King, 1975, 1978).

I said that autism has its origins in the earliest months of infancy. The infant experiences "bonding dissonance" with its mother and has a primitive urge to escape. Unlike the infant who becomes schizophrenic, the pre-autistic child does not detach and does not go into a prototypal trance, but, being a creature that may have a genetic predisposition toward action, it struggles, stiffens or goes limp managing to manipulate its escape and to get put down. Having escaped from bonding dissonance with mother, and having no need to go into a hypnotic state, it never needs to develop delusions and hallucinations as an adult but pays a major price because it misses a good bonding experience. Its needs for bonding remain and are redirected toward the non-human environment and toward self- stimulation in what I called "substitutive symptoms," which are mainly responsible for the weird patterns of behavior characteristic of classical infantile autism. Here was a description of the *pathogenesis* of infantile autism, which meant that the mother might *not* have been the origin of bonding dissonance. It could well have originated in a child with genetic deficits in its responses to bonding. *Whether the origin was in the mother or in the child was irrelevant to my theory!* Therefore, in working with these families, I avoided any blame, pointing out only that the child "never really let you be a mother."

This may well be the case, judging from the recent discovery of differences in four different genes in comparison of autistic and normal infants.

## Brain Changes
### as a Result of Experience

Years ago, I was certain that these experiences must have had an effect on brain development and chemistry. But I was so busy that I never looked into the research on the subject. Finally, in 1993, I began to scan the literature for evidence that this was the case and, of course, came across the classical work already reported from research in the late 1950s and early 1960s. In reference to this work, I said that the experience of bonding dissonance in both schizophrenia and infantile autism was likely to cause physical changes in the brains of some or all of these patients, as was supported by research with rats, cats, monkeys and other mammals in the late '50s and early '60s (Bennett, *et al.*, 1964; Greenough, *et al.*, 1987; Wiesel and Hubel, 1963; and King, 1993, 1994, 1995). For example, rats living together with other rats in cages with an abundance of rat toys to play with had five areas of cortex that were significantly thicker in their neuropil than matched rats raised alone in cages with only a treadmill. Research continued to show that experience affected both the chemistry and the structure of the brain in research animals and was even beginning to find this to be true in humans (Huttenlocher, 1992). Therefore the finding that severe schizophrenia is often accompanied by enlarged ventricles in the brain was to be expected.

Recent publications on neurochemistry in schizophrenia have confirmed my idea that organic changes affect the neurochemistry that, in turn, affect the behavior of the patient and the patterns of schizophrenic symptoms. The patient's experience and withdrawal in the early weeks of life would therefore be likely to result in simplification of neural patterns because of the effect of bonding dissonance. To give a name to this process I have proposed what I call "**The Law of Biological Simplification,**" which states, "**Brain structure and chemistry tend to be reduced to the minimum complexities required for those activities they support.**"

I believe that this is my own unique idea, but it may well be an idea that is already recognized in the scientific literature.

[Muscles not used atrophy; bones not used develop osteoporosis; tendons not used tighten; skills not used are lost, etc. So, a recent report that some schizophrenic brains have an excess of scavenger cells is consistent with these ideas. Nikkila, H. V., *et al.* 1999. "Accumulation of Macrophages in the CSF of Schizophrenic Patients during Acute Psychotic Episodes." *American Journal of Psychiatry* 156:1725-1729. More recent reports are especially interesting, in that schizophrenic brains were found to have no deficit of neurons themselves, but rather have what appear to be dendritic deficiencies. They show neuropil deficiency, meaning that the richness of the connections between the neurons themselves appears to be impoverished (Selemon, L. D. [2000]). ("A Measured Milestone in Schizophrenia Research." *Archives of General Psychiatry* 7:74-75; Glantz, L. A., and Lewis, D. A. "Decreased Dendritic Spine Density on Prefrontal Cortical Pyramidal Neurons in Schizophrenia" *Archives of General Psychiatry* 57 [2000]: 65-72.)]

A reverse corollary to this is the fact that "**biological complexity increases when it is useful to the function, survival or reproduction of the organism.**"

[In a letter to the *Los Angeles Times* regarding an increase in autism, I wrote,

> It is no surprise that the rate of autism is rising (*Los Angeles Times*, April 16, 1999). My research, beginning in the mid-1950s, addressed schizophrenia and autism. I saw what I called "bonding dissonance" between mother and infant as crucial to the development of both disorders. The child who later becomes schizophrenic escapes psychologically from bonding dissonance by withdrawal into a primitive state of "trance" between birth and seven months of age. Later it responds to stress by self-hypnosis to create schizophrenic symptoms.
>
> The child who becomes autistic escapes physically from bonding dissonance by struggling or going limp when held. It gets put down and uses the non- human world to substitute for its needs for nurture. That is the interaction the infant senses and reacts to after birth. Its behavior results in changes in brain anatomy and chemistry. Don't blame poor mother. She is doing the best she can in the mix she is presented with. The increase in autism is probably because technology and the means of communication have impacted on the mother-infant dyad. I expect the rate of schizophrenia will increase too, but it will take another one or two decades to see it …. (Unfortunately) psychiatry … is fixed on the idea that these illnesses are "just in the genes."]

I have repeatedly expressed and written my ideas thinking they were valid and important, yet often it has taken years for my writings to be published. Some never have been published. One of the reasons is that editors believed I was saying that the children who become either schizophrenic or autistic suffered from *deprivation* instead of the peculiar, specific experience of "bonding dissonance" between a particular mother with a particular child at a particular period of time. In addition, it may reflect a reaction by editors opposing the formulations by Freud and other psychoanalysts who were accused, erroneously, of not being "scientific." To me this seemed especially ironic, for I had decided in medical school to bring statistical methods with control groups and double blind experiments into psychiatry and had begun doing so in my first research and my first papers. Because there was such a desperate need for careful research design, others also utilized these methods, and, by the early 1960s, they were characteristic of much of the research in psychiatry.

The attitude that "science" should be limited to numbers derived from measurements is something Freud discussed on many occasions. Of course, measurements and numbers are crucial to science, but also crucial are observations and recording them. It was ironic to me to see the contortions some reviewers of my papers went through in order to justify rejecting them. They expressed difficulty accepting and even understanding my idea that the infant who experienced "bonding dissonance" detached and blurred out its focus of beginning awareness. I expressed this idea in a variety of ways and also referred to earlier papers in which I had taken what I thought were great pains to clarify it.

The gist of the reasons for rejection was that other reported observations on the families of schizophrenics found very little or no psychopathology. These observations were on gross patterns of behavior in families that were selected long past the patient's infancy. The crucial, subtle observations I called for were on particular mother-infant dyads during the specific period between birth and seven months of age.

Questioning the parents of these children after they have become schizophrenic often provides very little information. First, some talk about the patient's childhood as if it started at ten years of age. Second, people who seem blind to certain aspects of communication may talk about what a wonderful child the patient had been between birth and six or seven months of age. It is like trying to talk with people of conviction regarding religion and politics. I am reminded of the mother of a schizophrenic man who had auditory hallucinations regardless of large doses of clozapine. The mother actually said how "blessed" and "lucky" she was that her son had never used any drugs or alcohol, conveying that using drugs would be much worse than his schizophrenia in which he is almost totally crippled functionally.

I would love to have a time-space machine in order to monitor mother-infant dyads during those crucial early months. Most researchers have looked *too late* into the early family interactions and thereby tend to focus on the distortions that abound in those earliest relationships. Testimony to the fact that this truth can be missed is furnished by the denial of abuse by the medical profession, which never really admitted that parents can seriously injure a child until 1962, when the article on the *"battered child"* appeared in the Journal of the American Medical Association (Kempe, C. H., Silverman, F. N., Steele, B. F., *et al.* "The Battered Child Syndrome." *Journal of the American Medical Association* 181 [1962]: 14-24).

Pressure from the pharmaceutical industry, the force of lay-groups like the National Association for the Mentally Ill (NAMI) and the changes in leadership within the field of psychiatry combined to affect a dramatic shift in the professional views on mental illness. No longer were psychological factors important in shaping the picture of major mental illnesses. Instead, the new, dogmatic view arose that major mental illness is *"organic"* in its origin and that it was unnecessary to look any further, which made it very difficult for me to publish my most recent work at the time connecting my earlier ideas with the studies on the effects of experience on brain structure and chemistry.

One reason may have been a reaction to the idea in the past that some of the professional people in the behavioral sciences unfairly blamed the parents of children who were severely ill. Objections to any such blame combined with the failure of therapy to reverse severe mental illness may have led to some misunderstanding of my work and active rejection of any work that even *hinted* that early input from the parent played a role in the genesis of severe mental illness.

In addition, the pharmaceutical industry makes billions of dollars from its sales of psychiatric medication. It publishes articles, tapes and journals mailed free of charge to many doctors, and industry advertising supports many of the expenses for psychiatric journals. It also pays for a good proportion of psychiatric education and gives a variety of stipends to many of the leaders in psychiatry. Pam (Pam, 1990) and others (Rakow, 1994) have documented evidence that this industry has interfered directly or indirectly with the editorial freedom of psychiatric publications.

[Does the pharmaceutical industry try to stifle behavioral explanations of mental illness that could interfere with the use and profitable sale of psychiatric medications? Could there be a "medical-industrial complex" paralleling President Eisenhower's "military-industrial complex?" Of course, I do not know.]

Experiential explanations are often rejected these days because they are considered *"politically incorrect."* Even in 1975, when I spoke in Philadelphia on my ideas regarding the development of infantile autism, several hundred people filled the room and spilled out into the hall, many of them parents of autistic children who belonged to the National Society for Autistic Children (N.S.A.C). They had come to jeer and mock me for ideas that outraged them and that they seemed to think were mine. They believed I was saying that autism was *caused* by the mother's treatment of the child, which was not accurate, although I did not exclude that idea in at least some cases.

That experience led to my attendance at a meeting of the N.S.A.C. later that year in San Diego in order to mingle with the parents. I called it a "field study" of the parents of autistic children, having collected a modest amount of information that was most interesting.

Nine months later, at a meeting of the American Psychiatric Association, Edward R. Ritvo, M.D., was the discussant of a paper I presented, but furnished no discussion whatsoever. Instead, he leaned on the podium, smiled like a "Cheshire cat" and said to the audience, "Those of you who have heard Dr. King's paper and believe autism is experiential in origin, raise your hands." A few people in the audience raised their hands.

Then he said, "Those of you who do *not* believe autism is experiential in its origin, raise your hands." Most of the audience raised their hands.

Dr. Ritvo smiled and sat down. He apparently thought I was saying that the mother *caused* the child to become autistic, instead of my actual point that the genesis of autism lay in the *interaction* from the "bonding dissonance" between the mother and the child, regardless of its origin. I was reminded of the reception of Freud's paper on hysteria to the physicians in Vienna, when the discussant pointed out that "hysteria" referred to the womb and, therefore, could not occur in men.

[Freud now gets more than his share of rejection. A newspaper column on dreams ("In Your Dreams," *Los Angeles Times*) has made absolutely *no* reference to Freud in the few times I have read it. I have summarized some of the most sensible statements Freud made in his *Interpretation of Dreams* (King, 1975), but it now appears that *it is politically incorrect even to refer to Freud*. A controversy emerged in the last decade because Freud had said that there may have been less actual sexual molestation than he had believed when he had initially written on the subject. Some modern writers *acted as if Freud had now totally rejected the idea that molestation occurred at all!* Many people became annoyed at Freud, especially women, because it seemed to discount the many instances of actual incest and sexual abuse that so many women (and others) have been subjected to. However the actual incidence of incest and sexual abuse is not relevant to Freud's point that was simply that, like reality, *fantasy* can also motivate behavior.]

## ALTRUISM AS A BASIC DRIVE

In 1982, I said that a "Giving Stance" was essential for psychotherapy to succeed in some cases of severe emotional illness (King, 1982). Moving from this point, I later suggested that altruism was a basic drive for humans.

Many dictionaries and other reference books present a black and white picture of altruism, in which it is seen as the opposite of egoism. "The interests of others rather than of the self can motivate an individual," says the *Columbia Encyclopedia*. This polarizes the issue, leaving little room for a concept that actually accepts a gradient of behavior from adversarial to collaborative.

It is very important to realize that altruism can include egoism and that one's genuine empathy for others may permit an egoistic connection — a consideration of others' needs in a way that is not at all self-sacrificing, but is like "one hand washing the other." It renders "us or them" conflicts unnecessary in many contexts and furnishes room for a collaborative relationship which can benefit everyone.

This view of altruism gives us an explanation as to why so many of our citizens take a vital and active interest in building or caring for our society's infrastructures, so that we may all enjoy the benefits of education, equality in the application of the law, museums, parks, protection, transportation, *et al.* The fact that these things exist is testimony to my idea that relatively mature people have a *natural* impulse to practice altruism in this wider sense. Marmor and Gorney approached this point in their paper, which argued that aggression was not a primary drive (Marmor and Gorney, 1999).

An adversarial position was expressed at a course I once attended on the handling of prisoners in a correctional institution. The speaker said,

"You *can* use deadly force when there is an immediate threat of severe injury or death to another person." I asked if it was not just *permissible,* but also a *responsibility,* to use force in such a situation. Not just that you *"may,"* but you *"shall,"* to the best of your ability. The speaker was confused by my question, and I had to repeat it several times before he answered, "Yes there was such a responsibility."

I realized that his confusion was because he had assumed that correctional officers were like pit bulls straining at the leash to attack and only needed to be given the signal. I am capable of using force and have, but it is apparently not common for doctors and other non- custody personnel to feel any wish to use deadly force at any time.

## COMPLETION AND CREDIT AS BASIC NEEDS

Emerging from my ideas on altruism in 1990 was my notion that people have a basic desire to complete things, an idea original with me that others may have had too.

[Close to this idea was an ad for Qualcomm in *PC Magazine* (Vol. 18 [November 2, 1999]: 78) printed backwards, which said, "It's human nature to want to figure things out." When I developed this idea, I realized that it was natural for people to want credit for the things they accomplished and, in addition, to see others get proper credit for the things they did.]

When someone interferes with your attempt to figure things out, you are likely to get frustrated or upset in other ways. That is why people who have worked long and hard on tasks, or even pursued ideals, may get depressed when they cannot finish their work, especially people who seem to have high moral standards. But when you have accomplished that work, it may be equally frustrating to fail to get credit for it.

[An example of both of these points was given by a friend of mine, who said that it was like someone else telling the punch line to a joke before you have finished telling it. An illustration of the high moral standards among some depressed patients is presented by the patient I was treating who needed and received a "top security" clearance for his government work in the late 1960s. I had been contacted by a security agency, like the F.B.I., and asked whether his depression made him a security risk. I pointed out that just the opposite was true and that depressed people are often more likely than average to be conscientious and loyal.]

In other words, people who are conscientious about their work are likely to become frustrated and even depressed when someone or something interferes with the successful completion of their tasks. Normality entails a wide spectrum of behavior, and we expect most people to be cautious about getting cheated, nervous about competition, sad at the loss of a loved one, guilty about doing something bad and angry if someone does something hostile to them. However, when these feelings go to an abnormal extreme, as in the case of paranoia, panic, depression or murderous acts, psychiatric evaluation is warranted.

In the case of depression, *loss* is a major issue. Many psychiatric symptoms are found along a kind of gradient of loss. Anxiety is the fear of losing something valuable to you, like the respect of others, your money, your job, your freedom or your life (through earthquake, flood, flying in a plane, being robbed, etc.). Anxiety is often warded off by certain counter-symptoms. For example, avoiding areas haunted by spiders may keep the phobic fear of spiders and/or the anxiety of being bitten by a spider, in check; or obsessive-compulsive symptoms, such as repeatedly washing the hands, permits one to be busily engaged in an activity which creates the illusion of having some power over a cruel, impersonal, depriving environment.

***Loss and its vicissitudes may be basic to all psychiatric symptoms.***

Most psychiatric symptoms can be seen to work as a way to control anxiety one way or another. When people actually lose something or someone they love, they feel grief or mourning which may last for three to six months or more. A deeper sense of loss occurs in the case of depression. Often the loss may not be real, but actually exists in deep, hidden layers of the mind. For example, a multi-millionaire patient of mine had actually increased his wealth, but was crying that his financial growth had not kept pace with inflation.

Prolonged depression may become despair. Infants separated from their parents may die of loss in "hospitalism" and "anaclitic depression" (Spitz, 1957). At separation, infants may cry and be angry with their parents, and this serves as a useful "Darwinian" reminder to parents not to leave children alone and to take proper care of them. Even dogs act unfriendly to their owners, lurking in corners and avoiding eye contact for several days, after they are returned from the kennels where they have been left during their owners' vacations. Long after separation, a child viewing a film of being sent to the hospital slapped her mother's leg and called her a "bad mommy" for leaving her in the hospital. (Bowlby, 1963). Obviously, caring parents will think carefully about leaving their children alone again.

A sense of loss also occurs even when people fail to get credit for things they believe that they have done well. Because conscientious people tend to do things very well, it is not surprising that they are often more likely to develop depression. In addition, most people want to see others get proper credit for what they have done, provided they are not too demanding in their desire for attention. That's why we love heroes, especially those who are good, mature and exercise authority well. We feel good-hearted pleasure when we become aware of them and love to see them receive credit for things they have accomplished. Luckily there are many such heroes in history who come to mind, including those in the struggles against tyranny, bigotry and destruction of our environment. This love and appreciation for heroic acts is also reflected in our enthusiasm for the heroes of history, fiction, plays, and movies and even in the comics.

Children and infantile adults may be distracted from pursuing their goals because of their immaturity. We often observe that deprived people are temperamental, impatient or infantile in some other way, which makes it difficult for them to concentrate on tasks, being uninterested in pursuing them. Or they may be able to pursue them, but cannot maintain their pursuit, often being incapable of keeping at tasks except intermittently and fleetingly. In determining such issues, it is very important to be objective, because superficial impressions may be incorrect.

[The following example illustrates this point. Among my interests while on the psychiatric faculty at U.C.L.A. Medical School was a statistical study I conducted on the work accomplished by the psychiatry residents. The results showed two extremes: the most productive resident (A) treated 150 patients, while the least productive resident (F) treated 67. Between these extremes were the rest of the residents, who averaged 100 patients. The patients were assigned at random.

Resident "F" seemed temperamental and immature to me, but he gave a show of being extremely busy, often arriving at the hospital breathless, his tie askew, and acting as if he carried the whole world in his hands. Except for me, the faculty was impressed with him and rated him highly. Although I was surprised when I discovered how low his actual results were, I already believed that "F"'s behavior was more histrionic than heroic.

In contrast, resident "A" quietly and methodically went about his work with an absence of fanfare. Apparently, his matter-of-fact manner caused the rest of the faculty to see him as mediocre and plodding. Also, to my surprise, the actual results showed that this quiet, "plodding" resident "A" treated the most patients, finished their treatment in the shortest time and had the fewest patients need to return to the hospital, while Resident "F" treated the fewest patients, used the longest time to finish their treatment and had the largest number of patients needing to return to the hospital.

Resident "F" lost his license to practice medicine in the state about ten years after finishing his residency. Resident "A," whose name is Alvin

Pouissaint, M.D., joined the faculty at Harvard Medical School, was active with the civil rights workers in the South in the early '60s and later became a dean at Harvard and the consultant for the Bill Cosby show, because he was liked and highly respected by Cosby for his work. At times he appears on TV as a consultant on violence.]

Aristotle's philosophy is relevant to this issue of excellence in behavior. He classified people into three types: 1) those who seek only "contentment," *i.e.,* the "ordinary people" who are satisfied to have food, shelter, love and comfort; 2) the "politicians," who want contentment, but also want recognition and approval by the masses; and 3) the "philosophers," who seek truth and understanding. But philosophers also want recognition as well as comfort, and, if they do not get them, even they will be unhappy. Aristotle seems accurate regarding "philosophers," in that they want more than just the satisfaction of discovering truth. They also want recognition and contentment.

But Aristotle seemed to ignore the idea that *most people want more from life than just contentment.* In his day, ordinary people were probably so involved with surviving that it was difficult even for Aristotle to see the complexity of their needs. I think most people feel empty with a life that consists only of pleasure and contentment, although they may never have been consciously aware of it and never dreamed that they could accomplish more than they do. Yet every day we see people who somehow do gain fame and fortune develop the ambition to do something more. Often, actors who are popular in a particular role express dissatisfaction at being typecast, try to get roles different from those that made them famous, try to become writers or directors, or retire from acting. Does this mean that people are inherently dissatisfied with their lot, whatever it is, or does it mean only that they need more challenge?

Of course people who are addicted to immediate gratification are probably psychologically immature and less likely to feel satisfied. Certainly everyone is tempted to some extent by immediate gratification, but not to an excessive degree. For example, most of us love to eat, but few of us weigh more than 300 pounds. Certainly people have a wide range of interests, and many of them achieve admirable accomplishments, especially when they are persistent in mastering special skills. But I believe that mature people want more than mere satisfaction, and, therefore, I am not satisfied with Aristotle on this issue.

[What about those few people who deprive themselves, such as ascetics who engage in major suffering? Are they mocking us for our own temptations? Are they trying to counter — to go the opposite from — their own inner and powerful temptations? Or do they enjoy a kind of bragging advertisement for their own habits of self- discipline?]

Slightly different from this issue is what Freud wrote as almost an aside in *Formulations Regarding the Two Principles in Mental Functioning* (Freud, 1955) that artists and performers may so charm others away from harsh reality and responsibilities that they may have considerable success in gaining popular attention. Their seeming carefree, free-spirited, even reckless lives are often a mask covering years of study, hard work and selfless dedication that succeeds in luring us into the belief that the "artist 's life" is a "bowl of cherries."

Many actors, artists and athletes often have an easier time today than ever before. They often need not work so hard to gain attention, financial success and the adoration that used to be directed toward more serious endeavors. The media of communication seem to highlight the abundance of such successes, thereby contributing to the erroneous idea that knowledge and hard work are not necessary for success in anything. It often seems that the media wish to create an audience in which criticism and excellence are held in contempt.

Abraham Maslow used the term "self-actualization" to describe the advanced goals people are able to pursue once their more basic needs are met. Maslow went on to say that basic needs and their substitutes can chronically overshadow the pursuit of more advanced activities, leaving the individual with an ongoing sense of unfulfillment (Maslow,

1954). Psychoanalysts had addressed such issues in some detail for many years (Fenichel, 1945). They were incorporated by psychiatry under the concept of "personality traits" in 1952 (American Psychiatric Association, 1952) and, most recently, as "personality disorders" (American Psychiatric Association, 1994).

I think that *mature adults* prove to be relatively free of the usual inhibitions and constraints of society, yet are also free to adhere to them, if they choose. One of my sons said once, "Whatever happens is what I want to happen." But often we accept as "just what we wanted" that which just happens to turn up.

## THE RELATIVITY OF TIME AND THE KING POSTULATE

Once while in medical school, I experimented with marijuana. In the process, several strange and unique things happened as I became increasingly stoned. My skin seemed to melt. My kiss felt like my lips were melting and beginning to ooze and slide into my partner's lips. Time slowed until it seemed to almost stop. I glanced at my watch and it took what seemed like twelve months for the next ten seconds to elapse. I hallucinated that the people around me had frozen and were gradually being laced together with cobwebs. Then, I seemed to drift away slowly. I had passed out.

When I revived hours later and the party was over, I surmised that the process of the sexual orgasm would probably give me an "eternity" of pleasure. Shortly after that first experience, I neatly arranged to have sex with a very willing young doctor while we both got stoned on marijuana. It was marvelous at first. She had three or four orgasms just as the marijuana began to take effect.

But then, when I decided to ejaculate, it was a different story. After what felt like weeks of effort, I gradually approached my climax that was like the "big bang" of the universe! It seemed vast and profound and as if it had happened to me before, like the subconscious memory of the pangs at my own birth — violent pressure, intense pain, gasping, suffocating, blinded by dazzling lights, but in infinite silence. It lasted an eternity, but ended with a final release – a sudden explosion into comfort and peace.

Sigmund Freud saw birth as a significant stress that people overcame. Otto Rank (1929) saw birth trauma as a major issue in his book, *The Trauma of Birth*. But neither of them explained why birth had such a traumatic effect. My remembrance of what may have been my own seemingly eternal birth perhaps offers a reasonable explanation.

The subjective sense of time is entirely relative and the few hours it takes to be born must seem like an eternity to the infant. Could that one hour to a one-hour-old infant be like one year to a one-year-old child? The pressure, change of state and lack of oxygen during birth would seem never-ending to the child, making it a crucial experience of stress and fear that finally subsides. This type of relativity in the duration of time and space led me decades ago to ideas which I have written down recently and now call the **"King Postulate:"**

The realm of pure, abstract mathematics on the one hand and the realms of the science of reality — physics and astrophysics — on the other hand, have often been seen as two separate, seemingly divergent endeavors. But very often, advanced and abstract and "useless" mathematical methods have repeatedly proved to be the underpinning of some cutting edge physical theories, such as the use of the "Lorentz-Fitzgerald Contraction" by Einstein's in his theories of relativity.

Because of the fact that all — or so very many — seemingly "useless" mathematical representations have later proven to be keys to the workings of our universe, I state this theme:

**Every valid mathematical equation actually exists in reality and represents reality in some part of the extended universe — whatever that universe is. Included in that universe is the presence of time as a fabric that can be traversed in any direction. Thus time, space**

**and every dimension all exist at this moment and every moment and place: whenever, wherever or whatever — past, present, and future.**

## KING ARTHUR'S SWORD

My final impetus toward query and discovery was furnished by Professor Ward Halstead at The University of Chicago. When we started classes the first year of medical school, we were given intelligence tests, but were permitted only one-half the normal time to complete them. We were a bright group of students with IQ's mostly 140 and above and some of us were as young as seventeen. However I was the only student to complete all of the tests within the time allowed.

Then, during the following summer, I was invited to take some special tests given by Halstead's psychological lab to check "biological intelligence." Previously I had avoided trying to learn anything about intelligence tests, wanting to get a "true" picture of myself if I was ever tested. The Halstead tests were fun and like tests I had taken in the U. S. Army Air Forces, where I believe I scored higher than anyone else.

The Halstead tests lasted several days, and, after they were over, I was asked to meet with Dr. Halstead. I walked in and saw this commanding, gray-haired man sitting at his desk with his head down. He sat there silently for several minutes as I became increasingly intimidated and wondered if I had done something wrong.

Finally he asked me, "Are you King?" After admitting I was, he said, *"I'd give my right arm for your brain!"*

He said that I had done so well on his tests of "biological intelligence" that it would probably take another five years of testing University of Chicago medical students to find one as bright as I. In addition, I had shown an extremely high "power factor." To illustrate, he described the "flicker fusion" test in which the frequency of a blinking light is increased until it seems steady. I had detected an extremely high frequency and had repeatedly come to almost the same frequency with each trial. He said that my accuracy and perception combined with my intelligence were most remarkable and that I could achieve almost anything I wanted.

He added that I would be right most of the time in my views and choices and, as a consequence, was destined to experience frustration throughout my life. He wanted to test me every five to ten years to see what happened to me over time.

I was almost overwhelmed by this information. It reinforced my early ideas that I was different, somehow, like a visitor to earth from outer space. It confirmed my sense of confidence in what I believed was true and fair. It cemented in me the drive to pursue truth and understanding regardless of whether there was any God, any "plan" to the universe or any personal suffering and pain. Even whether there actually was any reality was irrelevant, because its mere *possibility* was sufficient within itself. Here converged in me all I had studied, all I had felt and all I had been told by my mother of somehow being an instrument of God — yet God was not necessary to my charge! Like an actual "King Arthur" as he pulled the sword from the stone, I knew my destiny. Dr. Halstead died ten years later, before I had a chance to return to him for further testing and examination.

My experiences have helped equip me for my lifelong pursuit of the Truth. In late adolescence and early adulthood I read many authors, including much of Freud. Motivated by Freud's self-analysis, I decided to force myself to think every thought and experience every feeling, no matter how depressing, embarrassing, exciting, frightening, guilt-provoking, and infuriating or whatever as a kind of emotional bodybuilding somehow magically combined with dream self-analysis. The harder it was, the more I forced myself mercilessly to confront each feeling and thought. I would experience a gamut of horrible things, like being buried alive in sand with ants eating my eyes, crawling in my mouth and choking me as I attempted to breathe. I plunged my soul deep into the smell of the ants, the taste of them as I chewed on them, the feel of them as they crawled into my mouth and my rectum, the sound of their high pitched voices in deafening unison, the itching sensation on all of my skin as they crawled over me and the panicky feeling of being totally immobilized and squeezed tight by the intense pressure of those billion grains of sand.

Most of my early adulthood after receiving my medical degree was spent learning adult, adolescent and child psychiatry and psychoanalysis. In addition to my seven years of university courses and supervision, I underwent about five years in formal analysis under my training analyst's supervision — "on the couch" four times a week. Then, several years after completing this psychoanalysis, I spent another five years as a participant in group psychotherapy for one and one-half hours once a week with about seven other colleagues under the leadership of Martin Grotjahn, M.D. All in all, I have spent more than 120,000 hours evaluating and treating my psychiatric patients. It has been a lifelong process.

In the following chapters, I attempt to disassemble the machinery that composes me – that makes me tick — looking at its cogs and wheels, exploring its functions and its inner workings.

*Dr. King's childhood with parents*

# Chapter III
## Beginnings

My mother was considered an exceptional beauty and my father, a handsome "Rudolf Valentino." They read the latest Aldous Huxley book as soon as it appeared in print. Their friends were talented young writers and artists. They were both brilliant, charming and athletic in those early days when I was born. They loved each other; they both loved me; and I loved them. My mother even smelled good, and I loved to bury my little nose in her hair and breathe in its special fragrance. My father seemed infinitely strong to me, and I loved to have him rub my face with his dashing mustache as he held me.

Jane, my mother, was born on March 24, 1906 and was still just 20 at my birth on February 20, 1927. My father, Ralph, was born in September 1905. My mother may have been uncomfortable with my being conceived before her marriage, but it seemed not to interfere in the least with her bonding with me. I was totally comfortable with her and with my father in those years. In our many family photos, in all of my rich childhood memories and in all my interrelations with my parents, I seemed to be entirely without conflict with them. Our earliest memories reflect the nature of our earliest environment.

I can remember and can still sense the complete love provided by my parents and their most attentive nurturing of me, even as I took my first tentative steps on the day I turned eleven months of age. I can actually visualize that moment. I was standing. My mother was holding me from behind enabling me to stand, her hands holding my little hands. My father was right there, crouched in front of me, holding out his two thumbs. I let go of my mother's hands — and I walked across to my father — and I grabbed his thumbs — and both my parents laughed with pleasure and lavished praise on me for my very first steps.

I have always carried an image of this experience in my mind. It includes the shape, colors and furniture of the room, the positioning of my parents and the intense light streaming into the windows.

When I first described this earliest image to my mother, she advised me, "Yes, Peter, that was the day that you took your very first steps, the day that you first walked."

Sometime after my birth and after my mother had completed her studies at The Art Institute of Chicago, she began an association with two very notable magazines in those days, *Vanity Fair* and *The Chicagoan*. She illustrated a number of the articles in *Vanity Fair* and in her column in *The Chicagoan,* she wrote a series of brief biographies of historically famous Chicagoans. Adjoining each biographical sketch was her perceptive caricature of the person. The entire set of sketches and caricatures remains with the Chicago Historical Society.

My mother was a most disciplined person and set a strict schedule for the two of us. Every morning at eight we were together for breakfast (I ate what I called my "bah-boo"). From nine to noon she usually took me the short distance over to the beach on Lake Michigan in the summer or just to nearby East End Park the rest of the year. Of course, I was chauffeured around in my stroller those very early years.

We had lunch from noon until one, but from one to five she was completely cloistered away in her study with the door closed. I was shut out and forbidden to interfere in any way with her writing or her painting, "no matter what." She told me that I should imagine that she had gone to downtown Chicago and was away there for the rest of the afternoon.

*Father with his nuclear family*

I recall adhering to mother's need for privacy to work religiously. So, generally I was entirely on my own and kept busy with all sorts of little boy activities. I did interrupt her once, quite violently, when our gas range exploded in flames. I had decided to do some "baking" and had my complex mix of flour, sugar and water just ready to cook on the range. The gas was on, but I had failed to push the starter flame button. The sudden explosion blew flour, sugar and water all over my face and brought my mother racing out of her study to see what had happened. She did not even scold me in that episode, perhaps having seen the humor and the justice in my endeavor to be constructively busy. She was clearly concerned for my welfare, but able to laugh about it and tease me in her sweet way about my cooking experiment and my look of total bewilderment on my slightly singed face.

In those days, I never saw anything mean in either my mother or father. They always seemed patient, constructive, loving and fair. Perhaps that explains my look of complete self-satisfaction in all my baby pictures and my growing sense of fairness to other little children, including even, several years later, my little brother Tommy. Around that time, I established the law, *"The sibling who cuts the cake should not get the first choice."*

We moved to a new, larger apartment in Chicago when I was about two or three. It was around that time when I first discovered that some people could be mean and cruel. Some rather rough little children lived on the next city block from us. I was walking there alone, slapping my hands in front of and behind myself and singing a childish ditty, feeling altogether quite satisfied with everything when several young "ruffians" spotted me. One of them, a year or so older than I, came right up to me and abruptly slapped me across the face. I was frightened, turned about quickly and ran like hell. Even now, at my very mature age, mean spiritedness in people still comes as a complete surprise to me.

People's dishonesty also remains a surprise to me. An older cousin and I often played together around our Aunt Kate's hotel back in 1933, when I was about six. We formed several clubs, one of which we named the "detective" club. We suspected that a hotel employee had stolen my wallet from a cigar box, which we had hidden in the hotel basement. Being novice detectives, we began a search of all the hotel employees' lockers and soon found some of my wallet's contents in the locker of a bellboy named Ben. We asked him very politely to return my wallet and, a day or so later, he tossed it across to the area of the side lobby of the hotel where my cousin and I were sitting. My cousin promptly picked it up and stated, "This is MY wallet!" I couldn't believe him. He was lying, and I was furious with him. I grabbed the wallet away from him, opened a small compartment and found a paper with my name on it. When I showed this paper to him, he retracted his lie and acknowledged that the wallet was mine. Of course, at the time, I might not have realized that my older cousin was just teasing me.

Not long after the birth of my brother Tom in 1931, I had to be hospitalized for a most severe infection. I was told later that for two entire weeks I had a fever that often hit as high as 108F. Two other boys in the same hospital with the same kind of infection had died. I was free of any illness, even colds, at that time so I had no or little resistance to combat the infection. My illness was particularly disturbing to my parents, especially my mother, who later conveyed to me how devastated she would have been to lose me. Losing any child would be a terrible tragedy to a parent. My early death would have been especially hard because, to my parents, I was smart, responsive and fun. I was a little "pal" to both of them and they recognized that I considered them to be my "heroes."

I looked forward to my brother's birth and was delighted when he arrived. He became increasingly cute and cheerful as he got older, and I used to tiptoe in to watch him sleeping in his crib at about 6:30 a.m. As he awakened, he would smile up at me and start hopping up and down in his crib in glee that I cared for him. This produced a special lifelong connection between us.

My father was something of a joker in his early years. He had been a rather difficult boy before his marriage and had been shipped off to the Wentworth Military Academy for his early education, probably to get "straightened out." One day in 1933, at his first well paying job, he received a phone call from a man he thought was just one of his other co-workers. He jokingly pretended that he was the "big boss" — the manager — and began to tease the guy on the line. But, that guy on the line actually was the boss, who promptly ordered my father into his office and fired him. This incident happened in the depths of the Depression, when a job was almost unobtainable. My mother's father, the manager of the Hyde Park Hotel in Chicago at the time, hired my father, his son-in-law, as a desk clerk.

My father had been very bright, handsome, strong and ambitious, yet he was something of a dreamer, wanting to be a millionaire with a yacht without having to work for it. During his adolescence, he had assembled crystal radios, learned the Morse code and aspired to be an inventor. It looked like he'd be a fine success. But having the responsibility of supporting a wife and two children, and then losing his job and having to become a "lowly" desk clerk in his wife's family's hotel must have kind of crushed him. From then on he began to drink and soon was consuming at least a fifth of bourbon whiskey daily. In spite of the liquor, he was up every morning and apparently never missed a day of work.

I gradually became unhappy with his lack of attention to me and increased withdrawal. He began to ignore me and stopped playing with me. I would beg, "Daddy, please play ball with me," or, "Daddy, please take me to the park." But he just sat in his chair avoiding eye contact and responded, "Later — maybe." My father began to ignore my little brother almost totally, which may well have contributed to his homosexual orientation later on.

By the time I was eight years old, my father, who worked at the hotel from 7 a.m. to 3 p.m., usually stopped after work at "Jimmy's," a saloon on Lake Park Avenue near the hotel. He'd spend some three or four hours over his booze. One payday, my mother, in desperation sent me to Jimmy's to get our dad to come home before his money was gone. I did not want to go, but I forced myself to do it. I have always been the kind of person who is able to do something even when I was almost totally opposed to or afraid of doing it.

On that beautiful, sunny, summer day, I pushed open the heavy saloon door and entered into the almost complete darkness of the place. I still recall the acrid smell of beer, the dank air, the silence and finally that dim vision of my father perched up all alone at the end of the long bar.

I went up to him and said, "Daddy, please come home!" He paid no attention, and several times I repeated, *"Daddy, please, please come home!"*

The situation continued to worsen. My mother couldn't write; she couldn't paint, she didn't know what to do. She ultimately suffered a complete nervous collapse. An awful, deep bitterness between my parents became a permanent aspect of our lives. A few years later, when he went off to work in Greece and failed to send back any financial support, she divorced him for abandonment.

I was just 18 the last time I saw my father. He contacted me when I was in Denver serving in the U.S. Army Air Force. I entered his hotel room and immediately saw an open fifth of bourbon on his dresser. He saw me stare at it and said, "Yes, I'm a drinking man." I felt extremely uncomfortable and believe I was feeling his discomfort, too. He took me out to dinner and to a football game. Since that time, whenever I am on a bus or subway, out on the street or in a bar and see an old man at the age he would be, I wonder, "Is that my dad?"

I prefer now to think of those earlier, happier days, before my parents' lives fell apart. I always loved summer and being at Lake Michigan with both my mother and father. My father could swim under water farther than anyone I ever knew, except for myself when I became older. I could swim under water farther than anyone at Camp Hoteling, our Episcopal Church summer camp in Twin Lakes, Michigan, or later on the high school swimming team.

[During college, after hyperventilating, I held my breath for more than eight minutes in competition with another premedical student, Jan Koch-Weser (he held his just shy of eight). Could we two have set a record back in 1949? I suspect not, because the Guinness Book of Records for 1977 shows the record as closer to fifteen minutes. My oxygen consumption with exercise on a stationary bicycle exceeded 6.9 liters per minute when I was 55, being 0.9 liters per minute greater than the "maximum" for men of all ages. In April 2000, it exceeded 5.99 liters per minute, still being greater than the "maximum" for men of all ages. I'm still in fantastic shape for a guy who suffered from polio, *et al.*]

Once, back in the 1930s, my father swam down underwater in Lake Michigan and hooked a little fish on my fishing line. The line consisted of a yo-yo as a bobber, a piece of string and an open safety pin as a fishhook. I was so proud when my mother said we would eat my fish for dinner. On our way home, she went into the fish market "to have Peter's fish cleaned." She came out with a package several times the size of my "catch" and explained to me how *incredible* it was that so much dinner could come from one little fish. For several years after that, like a little authority, I would say very seriously to other children, "It's incredible how much fish you get to eat from one small fish!"

Although very proud of myself for catching that family fish dinner, something about it didn't seem right to me. Finally, one day I told my mother this, and she, in turn, told me the real story. She had bought fresh fish from the market and they discarded the fish I caught. I was glad she told me and had no hard feelings, being grateful to have the mystery explained logically.

[As an adult, I work very hard to understand what people are trying to say and to obtain reasonable explanations for their ideas. Sometimes my family, my friends or my colleagues become impatient with me for attempting to pin down the exact import of their statements. My wife,

Simone, too, often says, *"You want to be right all the time — always the center of attention."* This frustrates me, but I just have to have my questions answered and issues clarified so I can completely understand it all.]

My mother was a good friend to me. From my earliest years we enjoyed talking with each other about art, our family, our friends, medicine, music, politics, religion, science, the stars, etc. It was a two-way street, and I openly and freely talked with her about almost anything. We both loved to gossip. Probably, those experiences also attracted me to psychiatry and helped me enjoy my work as a psychiatrist. I have almost never been bored by my patients and have usually found each to be an adventure in discovery. Each person is unique and special, just like his or her fingerprints. Perhaps this pleasure is the reason I have never suffered from burnout. I must admit, though, that I did fall asleep once while treating a patient, but that lapse occurred after my night of less than two hours of sleep.

As a youth and already having read many of Freud's writings and done my "emotional bodybuilding," I had an overwhelming desire to be psychoanalyzed in order to become a completely balanced person. To be intellectually quick and knowledgeable, physically strong and flexible, and emotionally mature and honest were very important to me. I was encouraged to have these traits by my mother, a wise, kind and patient person. However, when I brought home my high grades from school she told me to relax and not work too hard. She said, "Don't be too hard on yourself, Peter." This is quite the opposite of what other bright children might expect to hear if they get, say, five grades of A and one grade of B. They might hear, "Why didn't you get all A's?" As a result of this wise aspect of my upbringing, I have never suffered from burnout and I have retained my high ambitions and uncluttered motivations.

Also motivating me was the fact that I had nearly died four times. Life was a gift to me. I loved being alive, knowing, feeling, thinking, doing. The idea of dying was abhorrent. Early in my life I began to concentrate on maintaining a perfectly healthy body and was especially careful in eating, exercising and caring for all aspects of my health. I never felt suicidal and believe I would never kill myself. Despite that concern, I have been courageous, risked my life to save others and even gotten into fights over racial or religious bigotry.

[Once, a tattooed barber, a really big guy, complained to me about "kikes and niggers" while he was shaving my neck with a straight-edged razor. I cringed at his offensive phrase and said, "Don't you use language like that with me or anyone else!" He quickly apologized, saying, "Sorry, sir." Realizing how daring I'd been with that sharp tool of his so near, I quietly began to shake.

I had a similar experience in courage when I was an assistant professor of psychiatry at the U.C.L.A medical center. One day I abruptly tackled a six-foot, muscular, naked, psychotic young man who had become an immediate threat to us all, throwing him flat onto the floor.]

When I was in the Army Air Force and had just turned nineteen, I was stationed in the Hawaiian Islands. One day I went over and was watching, fully astonished at the huge and frightening winter waves of Makaha Beach on the north shore of Oahu. The waves were thundering down onto the sand, the wind was blowing violently, and megavolts of excitement sparked the air for the many spectators on the beach. Then I spied several young guys way out in the ocean catching those magnificent waves and surfing in on them. *I just had to ride those waves, too.*

With little thought of the danger, I got set with my surfboard and plunged right into the ocean. After catching a few smaller practice waves, I went out for a huge one, coming fast at me — it had to be a fifteen to twenty feet high! I attempted to align my body and board properly, but it was coming in faster than I'd thought and was dwarfing me. I caught it awkwardly, and the thrust of the wave crushed me into a ball and hurled me back and toward the beach. After crawling up out of the water, gasping for air and defeated, I yelled out, *"Oh God, I've broken my back!"*

For years after that episode, I had severe back pain, yet I continued to be active in all sports, regardless of the pain. Although I had always measured 5 feet 10½ inches in height after I was 18, I measured 5 feet 9¼ inches after being crushed by that wave. I thought the earlier measurement was in error, because I could not believe that I had really broken my back. However, about ten years ago an incidental x-ray of my back showed that I had crushed L1 and L2, obliterated the disk between them and lost about 1¼ inch in height. So I began to use more proper abdominal exercises. Instead of doing sit- ups sloping head down on a slant board with weights behind my head, I switched to abdominal crunches and supine elevations of my knees to my chin 60 times three days a week. Luckily now I remain fairly supple and almost totally free of any back pain.

TRIATHLON Long Beach- July 25/1983
Peter King: Won the first place in his age group 55-59
Time: 3 Hours /1/2

*Dr. King won the Triathlon his age group*

[This experience led me to modify an exercise table presented in Joseph Weider's *"Triple Progressive" Muscle Building Courses* (Copyright 1965), which illustrates symmetrical body development, in order to know which body parts need more exercise. I modified his table to calculate suggested dimensions more easily, permitting myself to retain my symmetry when I became bulkier and heavier as a younger man. As a result, I have remained close to the "ideal" for most of my adult life, whatever my weight and height. Below are the figures for my sixties, and, even now in my early seventies, I am close to them:

## Modified Exercise Table

| WEIGHT(#) = | CHEST(") | IDEAL | ACTUAL |
|---|---|---|---|
| A | 3. 37 | 37 | 37 |
| WAIST(") | (CHEST X .75) | 28 | 29.9 |
| HIPS | (CHEST X .9) | 33.5 | 34.5 |
| FOREARM | (CHEST X .3) | 11 | 11 |
| BICEPS | (CHEST X .36) | 13.3 | 13 |
| CALF | (CHEST X .36) | 13.3 | 13 |
| NECK | (CHEST X .383) | 14.2 | 14.5 |
| THIGH | (CHEST X .54) | 20 | 20 |
| BUILD | ( W T# / H T"- 143/68.5) | 2.1 | 2.1] |

Although I can work very hard and defer pleasure for long periods of time, I make a point of enjoying myself and relaxing whenever I can, even if it is just to put my feet up on a desk to read. It is as important to be nice to *myself,* as well as to other people. There are always tasks to be done, so I schedule each vacation well in advance and be sure to take it. I failed to take any vacations from childhood until 1964. From then on, I made an important point of getting away every year. But I usually return a day early to read the mail, tie up loose ends and prepare carefully for the return to work. I always prefer to be slightly early for work, meetings and even social events. It feels good, it's courteous, and gives me an illusion of leisure.

I always try to be nice to people not only because it makes a better world but also because it lets me feel good about myself. I am not trying to avoid guilt, because I seldom ever feel it. But it helps my self-esteem to be cheerful, forgiving and have good spirits. Even doing good things no one else ever sees or knows about helps me feel good about myself.

[Those people who are full of bitter complaints most of the time must be *optimists* at the deepest level. They must always be expecting something very good to happen. Otherwise, why are they complaining? In reverse, I am obviously a deeply committed *pessimist* because I am always (like Professor Higgins in *My Fair Lady*) so cheerful, good-spirited and almost never complain. I must be pleasantly surprised that things do work out when I was obviously expecting the worst. I need to clarify that this is a very serious position of mine that I have commented on for most of my life. Perhaps my near-death experiences forged deeply into my character the idea that there were strong chances that nothing would work out.]

[My fourth brush with death, which was very like my experience surfing in Hawaii earlier, occurred in Newport Beach in 1965 at the "wedge." I had been a strong swimmer and lifeguard, but, as a bystander, I had rescued or helped to rescue several people that day from the surf, which was most severe and later washed away a few houses. I decided to body surf in the huge waves, and, as I swam out, the tide began to come in. I was hit by one of the first waves. It broke both of my eardrums. The cold water rushing into my ears caused extreme vertigo, and I had no idea of what was up or down. All I could do was to hold my breath and roll into a ball until I broke the surface and took a breath. Wave after wave hit me, and I was beginning to lose my strength, but, as I was washed in closer to shore, I began to wave for help. The few people on shore who had seen me rescue others only waved back to me. Then, I was caught in the riptide and swept to the north toward worse currents. I was certain I would drown. Two young men recognized my need and managed to reach me and pull me out of the ocean. Tears welled up in my eyes as I thanked them with full conviction that they had saved my life.]

[Another close brush with "the grim reaper" occurred just last year (1999) when I was advised that I had a solid mass – a little larger than a golf ball— in the left lobe of my liver. I was scheduled for a biopsy later in the year and knew that the chance of my having hepatic cell cancer was high. My life expectancy could be as short as three or four months. With sadness and regret, I accepted my fate, perhaps like a soldier bravely going out into the battlefield knowing his chances of survival are slim. I felt surprised and proud of myself as I recognized that I was actually courageous. I would certainly regret leaving my family and friends. It was at that time that I accelerated my work on this book to be sure to finish it before I died.

But, I needed one more test before the biopsy. It turned out that I had a benign hemangioma of the liver, something that is not only fairly common, but also not malignant. The specialist told me to return in six months for more tests. I felt ecstatic because the lump was benign and lucky because a biopsy on a hemangioma in the liver could have caused me to bleed to death.]

In my childhood, I was free during school vacations, until I started to work by selling magazines and contributing occasional "loans" to my family to help out financially. From that time on through elementary school, I walked dogs, picked up trash and sang in our Episcopal Church choir. I always worked while I attended school and, in high school, I was a delivery boy, a grocery store clerk, and worked in a tailor shop, in a restaurant and a dress shop. I enjoyed working and gladly contributed to my family, feeling a sense of importance at being able to help out. Most people found me outgoing, cheerful, industrious and very grateful for anything given to me. I felt good and had good will toward others.

[Occasionally, though, some people seem to resent me. A young doctor on our staff at Madison State Hospital in 1959 said to me one day, in no uncertain terms, *"King, I don't like you!"*]

# Chapter IV
# A Little About Sex

Except for a crush on my mother when I was little, I am aware of no sexual or romantic memories before the age of five. During most of my childhood, I really did believe that mine was the best mother that could be and was surprised when other children said *their* mothers were the best. Sometimes I argued with them, but soon learned it got me nowhere and would just smile smugly to myself in the private notion of certainty that they were wrong. One day around the age of five, I realized that such things were relative and as a young adult, decided that the important issues were the feelings of trust, love and respect for a parent, regardless of any objective reality. I do not recall any Oedipal rivalry with my father. I openly respected and loved him in those early years almost as much as I respected and loved my mother. I was also delighted with my brother Tommy from the time of his birth until several years after that.

As Tommy got older and seemed to me to be rather slow and too often in need of our mother's help, I became annoyed. I was careful to use valid criteria and not to expect too much from him, but when he was being helped long after the age that I had no longer required any help, I complained that I had done those things much earlier. For example, I had tied *my* shoes before I was three, so I allowed him one extra year. Then, when mother was tying his shoes after he was *four*,

I permitted myself to complain. I kept careful track of dates and gave Tommy the year's leeway in order to have a legitimate complaint if he failed to tie his shoes on time.

Later, I targeted my mother with bitter complaints for failing to spank Tommy for things I would have been spanked for at his age. Her response was that we were two different boys with two different personalities requiring two different modes of treatment. She said that I was much more rebellious and argumentative than my little brother and that he was much more accommodating than I. Her comments were only annoying, and I went away pouting.

[Incidentally, I may make my brother sound only average, but he certainly was not. Before Tom was twelve years old, he began to take an unusually strong interest in mathematics and started studying calculus on his own. Later, when he was president of the Senior Mathematics Club at Hyde Park High School, he and his team were entered in the prestigious Chicago math contest. Tom and the team swept the top four prizes. Tom was upset at coming in second instead of first, but it helped him obtain a full scholarship to The University of Chicago, from which he obtained his master's degree in mathematics at the age of twenty. Tom then went east to pursue a Ph.D. in mathematics at New York University. He found the atmosphere there incompatible with the vast other pleasures New York City had to offer him, became an actuary instead and eventually was appointed vice-president of a prestigious Wall Street consulting firm.]

When I was five years old, a sixteen-year-old boy who lived upstairs began to molest me. Jackie played with my penis, had me touch his penis, and then used a vibrator on himself and me. It felt good and I enjoyed the sexual excitement, but it never gave me an orgasm. That happened almost once a week and, after some weeks, Jackie began to give me presents, including a golf club, a bugle, a dollar bill and some other items. Getting presents made me feel like something wasn't right about his attentions, and I began to feel guilt. After several months of this, my mother became suspicious and asked me if Jackie had ever "touched" me. I was evasive, but she was persistent. I finally started to cry and blurted out that he had touched my "weenie."

My mother confronted Jackie's parents about what their son had done, and they were shocked, each blaming the other. Meantime, I told some other children in the neighborhood about Jackie and just what had happened. A few days later a group of four or five of us went over to my Aunt's hotel, where Jackie was an elevator operator, and danced teasingly in front of him at his elevator, chanting over and over, *"JACKIE IS A NURTZ!"* He was embarrassed and humiliated. Soon afterward, he and his family moved away. The police were never informed, as they would have been today, but my hunch is that Jackie never did anything like that again.

I respect my mother for handling the issue quickly and effectively. Perhaps that is why that experience was never traumatic for me, as far as I know. I remained a fairly normal boy and never molested anyone. I was heterosexually oriented, except for the few usual exploratory experiences with other boys. My cousin and I talked a little about sexual things and watched each other touch our own "weenies." When I was ten, my cousin told me, under sworn secrecy, that babies were made by the father putting his penis into the mother's anus to plant a seed, which then caused a baby to start growing in the mother's stomach. We were both horrified at the idea that our parents had engaged in any such process, although neither of us dreamed that any *pleasure* might be involved.

When I was six, I fell in love with Barbara S., who was in my first grade class in the Kenwood elementary school. I worshipped her and would sit in class and look at her as if she were a work of art. Having no conscious sexual interest in her, I suspect that my love was a displacement of my love for my mother, whom I also worshipped. Both had pageboy, bobbed brown hair. My love for Barbara lasted until I was almost twelve.

[This love for Barbara S. was at the beginning of my puberty

63

and probably related to an indirect incestuous threat. My feelings were definite and strong, and, though it did not include an intimate friendship, I believe my intimate friendship with my mother must have colored it. The wish for such a complete and tender love has always remained with me, but I never experienced it to that extent again. I learned later that Barbara had a crush on me, but we were both too shy to approach the other.]

I had crushes on other girls and some older women. Then, at fifteen, I met one of my mother's first cousins, Janet Bard, who was in her mid-twenties. I fell deeply in love with her and was almost overwhelmed with outright sexual and physical desire. Her sister Katharine was a glamorous actress of much renown (and the wife of Martin Manulis, the producer of the *Playhouse 90* television series in the 1950s), but my crush was on Janet. Later, when I learned of her engagement to one of her handsome suitors, I was unabashedly rude to him. I inappropriately, but clearly, "wanted her for myself," with no reservations. Years later my mother's younger brother John told me that he had felt the same way about Janet.

[Janet's wealthy father, Ralph Bard, was a top executive and major stockholder of Eversharp-Schick Corporation and served as Undersecretary of the Navy during World War II. Before I received a full scholarship for medical school, he generously loaned me several thousand dollars for college tuition. Of course, in those "good old days," tuition at the private University of Chicago School of Medicine was only $900 a year. Of course, later I repaid everything I borrowed, which not all young people do.]

Being nice, good-looking and having a kind of friendly shyness, which I later was told added to my appeal, I was the object of attention of many girls. One little girl, Lillian, used to give me candy from her mother's store. We were both ten years old, and, not yet being able to ejaculate, I decided that she presented a great opportunity for me to have some "safe sex." My plan was to suggest she follow me to the basement and "have some fun." However, I never really got around to asking her.

Like many children, my curiosity about sex was strong, and I had the definite desire for intercourse with a girl. Yet, wanting to be a doctor and knowing that it would require a long course of study, I held back, being afraid of the shame of getting a girl pregnant and the responsibility of having to care for her and the baby. One extremely attractive girl, Patsy, made a date with me to "go out," which meant sex for sure to me. Feeling that this was a crossroad between good and bad, after pacing the streets for a half hour, I stood her up. Actually, I believe I was *afraid* to keep the date.

Later I was also afraid of becoming so attached to a girl that it might interfere with my embarking on a medical career. Consequently, my first real sex with a woman was not until I was 21 years old.

I discovered masturbation and had my first orgasm at the age of ten. A song at the time had words about "that old feeling," which I associated with the feeling I had with an orgasm, but I did not actually ejaculate until I was fourteen or fifteen. In keeping with my scientific bent, I kept records of the times I masturbated and ejaculated (and later I kept records of the times I had sex with someone). When I was fifteen, I spent the summer with my cousin John Cornell at our cousin's summer home in Newfane, Vermont. I had gone 30 days without masturbating. John expressed amazement and respect for my strength, but, one day he saw me come out of the bathroom after I had masturbated and said, *"You didn't!"* I sheepishly replied that I had, and he was most disappointed in me.

[Years ago I discovered that urologists use prostatic massage to treat acute and chronic prostatitis. The treatment was also believed to reduce the probability of benign prostatic hypertrophy and possibly prostate cancer. I decided to stimulate my own prostate gland in order to keep it healthy. Approximately once a month for about two minutes I would stimulate my prostate with a vibrator with an appliance for anal insertion.]

Was my record keeping of sexual episodes and other such things my attempt to control fear and anxiety? Looking back to the long hospitalization when I was only four, this recordkeeping may well have been an attempt to cope with loneliness and loss. At fifteen, as I was gradually becoming paralyzed with polio, I struggled to keep my throat clear. I strained to such an extent that my mother and the nurses admonished me to stop it, but I ignored them. In retrospect, clearing my throat that way was lifesaving. In addition, it was an attempt to engage in some action that would counteract my feelings of helplessness. Such behavior obviously helps survival by continuing the struggle, even when it seems hopeless to do so. Being in control, struggling relentlessly, pursuing an illusion of control and power, and possessing a sense of confidence that life must and will go on all have a powerful survival value consistent with evolutionary concepts to continue with our lives and procreation.

I had the notion that people had a responsibility to be good citizens, good parents and good spouses and thought it would be useful to teach those things in school. I also felt a duty to be clean, attractive and responsible. Later, as an adult, I felt an obligation to give a woman good sexual pleasure in a sexual relationship, and most of the women I was involved with sexually found me to be a good partner. I learned much from my belated sexual experiences with women, so the later Masters and Johnson (1966) work on human sexuality did not surprise me. My attitude toward women was colored by my relationship with my mother, so having been a "pal" to her permitted me to be a "pal" in my relationships with other women. Consequently, I was able to discuss what caused sexual pleasure and engage in some sexual experiments aimed at maximizing it.

On a few occasions, I had dates with women I met specifically for sex. We both enjoyed the sex, but I found that I wanted more than just a sexual relationship. I wanted long-range intimacy and friendship as well. That realization led me to decide that my desires represented the norm for a human male and that those who engaged in repeated changes in sexual partners were immature and fearful of permitting intimacy to develop. I think I had a natural respect for women. That may be why I turned down the opportunity for notoriety when Wolpert Productions wanted to use me in my work with patients and other activities in "the story of a psychiatrist" about five years before Toni Grant began her radio show. So, I might well have been the first of the media shrinks. However, I felt uncomfortable about using patients in ways that would compromise their privacy, so I turned down Wolpert Productions.

My practice of discussing sexuality and sexual pleasures with my partners gave me sufficient comfort to admit to myself what I believed were my sexual shortcomings. Many men and women require ample time – many episodes of sexual contact – before they can become fully comfortable with their partners and fully responsive to them sexually. My increasing comfort with sex allowed me to use a few alternate sexual methods as I became older. In my sixties I began to have difficulty getting and keeping an erection about 25% of the time. In my seventies this difficulty almost tripled. I learned to stimulate my wife in a variety of ways that brought her, sometimes again and again, to the verge of climax. Without specifying the details here, I have suggested the use of such techniques to older male patients, who have been delighted with their improved sexual relationships as a consequence.

When I was 21 and working as a student in the campus bookstore, an attractive, slightly older woman started to work there. Soon, she began to touch and fondle me when we were out of sight, back behind the bookshelves. Eventually she asked me to come over to her apartment to have sex with her. Her live-in "boyfriend" was out of town almost every weekend. For several months I went to her apartment each Saturday night and was treated to an abundance of sex. She was delighted to be the one to introduce me into the pleasures of sexual intercourse, including some exotic practices, such as "69."

We had some wonderful times, and it was a great experience for me sexually. Our relationship ended when she married her boyfriend, which was fine with me. I had just begun my pre-medical courses, was younger than she and had yet no interest in marriage. She was also a "loose woman" in my view. She had been involved sexually with several celebrities, one of whom Robert M. had been the most exciting lover she ever had. She loved to talk with me about her experiences and listen to me about mine. That candidness about sex proved to be an important aspect of my relationships with women prior to my first marriage at twenty-three.

[Was it also a clue as to how I handled any Oedipal wishes with my mother, that is, being a pal to my mother, getting into her good graces, but keeping sex completely taboo.]

I have had no homosexual experiences aside from being molested as a little boy by that older elevator boy and being present while several other boys masturbated together. I did engage in the usual boyhood comparison of penis sizes, but my interest was always in women and girls. As a youth, I longed to have a cute aunt or baby sitter who would have regular sex with me. I was also propositioned by several homosexual men, some of whom were annoyingly persistent, but I was always polite and firm in saying, "No way," to them.

During college, I began to give tips on ice-skating to a fellow student named "Neff," who had been a bomber pilot in World War II. One day he sent me several poems he had written declaring his deep love for me. When I told my mother about it, she insisted that if I did not punch him in the face I might as well be homosexual myself. I felt that this was the wrong way to treat the incident, but the next time he came up to me and handed me more poems, I brushed him off with a dramatic show of anger: *"Stay away from me or I'll break you in two."* He was so crestfallen, so heartbroken that I realized I had been too abrupt, too cruel. At that moment, I decided that my own judgment on issues should be trusted in all kinds of matters. I learned to depend on my natural good taste, judgment and intuition with full confidence.

# CHAPTER V

# EARLY YOUTH

### EARLY THOUGHTS

There had been several milestones in my early life when I made certain conscious generalizations about the world, myself or other humans. Some of those generalizations were just a mild awareness without full conscious realization or intent that I expected some specific pattern of behavior to recur. Later, especially after those same patterns arose consistently, my awareness sharpened to the realization that they were actually almost *always* going to recur, no matter what. In other words, I learned to trust my initial intuition. I also learned that *exceptions* to any set pattern could occur, permitting me to remain unbiased and objective about people and later, about my patients. I continued a process and habit of listening and gathering data before coming to conclusions about myself and people in general.

[I often fail in my manner to appear as a deliberate and cautious kind of person. In reality, I am quite the opposite. My exceptionally fast mental processing is beyond the comprehension of most people. I become confident of what is being said quickly, and I become eager to move on to what has not yet been covered or to some new aspects of the discussion. I become impatient with the slower mode of thinking of most other people.]

I gradually came to trust my observations and the conclusions that emerged from them. That trust was verified so often that I even learned to trust my intuitive hunches, which required gradual development. First, I had the conscious realization that what I predicted would actually happen. For example, when I was five, I realized that time seemed to move faster as I grew older and said to myself that I should expect this to continue to occur in the future.

Another example was my "ambition" to become a Boy Scout. At age nine, I had read the *Manual for Boys* and decided that Boy Scouts were indeed fine, moral and outstanding. When I became a Boy Scout at age twelve, I was keenly disappointed to find that scouts were only ordinary boys just like the others at school. I then said to myself that no matter what heights to which I should happen to rise in the world, I should expect to be disappointed in those who peopled those heights. Not surprisingly, that expectation was borne out. At the same time, I found many people who had extraordinary qualities of bravery, compassion, competence, genius and humanism, which made me proud to be a human and helped motivate me to do what I could to contribute to humanity, life, survival and universal peace.

The writings of Auguste Comte presented some very important insights for me. He termed "positivism" as the process of searching for invariant laws of both the natural and social world. The process is based on the premise that there *is* a real world and that the moral task of society is to discover and report on it. In that sense, the ideas in my book, *The Principle of Truth,* approach Comte's ideas. However, I differ from him in that I believe that merely *trying* to discover and report the truth is sufficient in itself as a philosophy of morality and quest. Nothing beyond the self need actually exist.

Comte also presented the idea that disorder in the world motivates "positivism" to seek order and progress, being a "spirit" which evolves from "human nature." Like what Spencer, Durkheim and I have written, Comte saw human progress as a movement from egoism toward altruism.

He seemed to see the emergence of that change as a natural result of the developing complexities of society and of the impact of those complexities on humankind. In essence, it was a natural result, like the emergence of a blossom from a plant.

Karl Marx viewed human progress as primarily economic at first, as it moves through capitalism toward a classless society relatively free of the need for production by workers. I tend to see human progress as a major product of the *maturation* of people and as a product of *increasing mental health* of individuals. Such progress is now rather uncertain, because an increasing proportion of our population lacks maturity, and we continue to remain in danger of destroying our world.

Society often reinforces the practice of altruism by acknowledging and even rewarding individual acts of altruism. Thus, individual, "natural" morality arises from each level — from the individual, the family, the culture and society at large. At each level, increased maturity accelerates the development of morality at all the other levels. In my view, our modern population has begun to lack proper bonding with their parents, families and outsiders. As a result, our society is beginning to lose its former humanism. People are bonding with computers, television, electronic games and CD-players as substitutes for human relationships.

My ideas and those of the sociologists I have mentioned here are not contradictory, even though each of us offers slightly different perspectives on the issues. One comment on my views needs to be made. More than the others, I believe that the individual is freer to act because of the "categorical imperative" and morality's reinforcement of self-esteem. On the other hand, I believe that the tendency to continue habits of behavior and thought marshals against action. Witness the power of tradition, religion and many individual behavioral patterns to interfere with or prevent any change in the habits of so many people. Of course, the development of habit is extremely important in facilitating survival. Imagine how impossible life would be if we had to think through every single aspect of an issue before acting. Yet, at times it is important to be free of habit, and those people who are able to change when it is very important to evoke our admiration.

In discussing Comte, Ritzer (Ritzer, 2000) was critical of the value of Comte's contributions, largely because Comte's later insanity and narcissism led him to present some ludicrous, totalitarian and megalomaniacal ideas. Ritzer also criticized Comte for his failure to gather facts to support his theories. Regarding this, because some truths are available from intuition, it is important to utilize, rather than neglect, intuition as a source of knowledge. We must then focus our attention on checking out the validity of our conclusions.

## SERVING OUR COUNTRY

When I was seventeen, I enlisted in the U.S. Army Air Corps "Enlisted Reserve," which enabled me to remain in high school for one more academic year. Although wanting to be a hot fighter pilot, I also wanted to continue my education as long as possible. Summoned to active duty, I went by way of Fort Sheridan, Illinois, to Keesler Field, Mississippi, for basic training. Being in third place among four hundred enlistees for flight training in physical fitness, as tested by pull-ups, push-ups, running and sit-ups, I had nearly overcome most of the effects of my past illnesses. I was also at the top in tests of coordination and intelligence. With me was a new friend, Roger Moister Des Prez, who also wanted to be a physician, but World War II ended and all chance of flight training was terminated. We were both sent off to Lowry Field, Denver, Colorado, to clerk-typist school. Roger and I became highly competitive with each other and engaged in many a duel of wit and intellect. Both of us declined the offer to attend West Point military academy, wanting to be discharged and attend college and medical school. Roger was sent to the Aleutian Islands, but I assured my discharge by re-enlisting for one year. I received a bonus, a month's leave and was discharged after serving first as a supply clerk, then later as supply "sergeant" for the Hawaiian Air Materials Area (HAMA) at Hickam Field, Oahu, Hawaii. In Hawaii I had many responsibilities in my job, competed with the Army Air Forces Pacific swimming team, worked as a lifeguard at Fort Weaver Beach and took a number of courses in mathematics, science and psychology. I wanted to learn as much *as reasonable*.

[I was committed to many different kinds of appealing activities at that time, but felt a responsibility to myself to engage in a variety of pleasures. It takes little to satisfy me and, knowing from personal experience that life can end at any moment, it seems wasteful of the gift of life not to take some appropriate time for pure pleasure. Such pleasure enriches me and also allows me to become a vehicle to carry the richness of my experience to others.

Robert Louis Stevenson conveyed that idea to me in his *The New Arabian Nights,* which I read it at age nine and resolved to read again (as a mature adult, though, I found it rather boring). The characters probably reflect in some ways the character of Stevenson himself, who, like me, also suffered from several near fatal illnesses. I believe that having such near-death experiences produces a natural sense of urgency in people, who subsequently cannot delay making decisions for long, but must act promptly in a wise and efficient manner. I decided early in my life that it is better to be right than wrong and better still to be right quickly rather than slowly.]

Having completed a G.E.D. test and scoring mostly at a 99+ percentile, I received my high school diploma and was accepted by The University of Chicago without an entrance exam. Luckily, I was eligible for three years of G.I. Bill education and support that was enough to finish pre-med and one quarter of medical school. Although working on the side 25 to 30 hours a week, I also took as many as 21 hours of courses a week. The placement tests at The University of Chicago allowed me to obtain a bachelor's degree with only seven courses.

Therefore, in three years I was able to work on and obtain two degrees, a B.S. and a B.A., and was able to start medical school.

I continued working during medical school between 25 and 50 hours a week. I held several jobs at once. I was a clerk at the university bookstore, a Fuller brush man and a dishwasher in a hospital laboratory. I became a laboratory technician in the hematology laboratory, testing for fecal and urinary urobilinogen, and later setting up a laboratory for research in blood coagulation.

Some of my research was published in two articles written with Carroll Spurling (Spurling, King, 1954). The articles said that antihemophilic globulin (AHG) was stoichiometric in its action, being like a building block which is used up, while the "Christmas factor," or "PTC," was catalytic, being a stimulant to the speed of blood coagulation without being used up much, if at all.

Understanding how something works is important to me. At that time I had some contempt for practical applications, reserving my highest respect for mathematical, astronomical, physical and philosophical theory. In my early days, that view was common among students, and those who went into "industry" by working in manufacturing instead of doing basic research and teaching were looked down on as selling out their idealism for materialistic gain.

# Chapter VI
# God, Poetry and
# Other Ideas

## God and Religion

Although I consider myself an agnostic, I have prayed many times. However, I feel a responsibility never to pray for my own success nor the success and health of those close to me in a selfish way. I do not want to *waste* my prayers on selfish things. *I reserve my prayers for the good of the world and for the survival of the human species.*

My good wishes, good will, good ambitions and the way I usually conduct myself all seem to attest to my being a good and noble person. Therefore, it is difficult for me to imagine that there is any God who is less humanistic than I.

If God were a vindictive creature damning those with the audacity to question his legitimacy or those who fail to follow slavishly his supposed directives (like the "religious right" and some extremist sects seem to think), I would be unable to admire or worship him. If there were a God, this God would have to be at least as liberal and humanistic as I.

[Many religious people are righteous in their beliefs, sincerely believing that the Bible (or the Torah, Koran or whatever) was actually written by God directly or by humans through some process of divine inspiration. They have no doubts on some matters, quoting the Bible as if it provided absolute proof. I do not agree with such views and do not want them to try to force such views on me. ]

[By the way, I use the word "God" alone to mean whatever *you* mean when *you* use that word. It is awkward to keep writing "God, if there is any actual God" or "God, if he, it or she actually exists." Notice that I use the personal pronouns in *alphabetical* order. Ever since the 1970s, when I read Betty Friedan's *The Feminine Mystique,* I have written in ways that usually do not require the use of personal pronouns, but when I do, I write or say them alphabetically, such as "for her or him," or "he and she entered the race." I find it frustrating when an editor changes my wording. So, don't think I actually do believe God exists, and if I refer to God as if it were a male, I do not wish to imply that God is likely to be of some sex or a computer, machine, force or whatever.]

Someone once wrote that questioning God is testimony to the excellence of creation and serves as an inherent compliment to a job well done. However, we poor humans are like two-dimensional creatures in a world of three, four, or more dimensions, lacking the ability to imagine the reality of a more extended universe. We are incompetent to do more than simply approach truths, much less speculate, or, worse still, legislate on such matters.

## NATURAL AUTHORITY

Because of my admiration for Robert Maynard Hutchins, whose ideas inspired me to attend The University of Chicago, my first son was named Dana Hutchins King. Like his older sister Katherine, Dana walked at seven months and was a bright, cheerful baby.

[The day Dana was brought home from the hospital after his birth, Kathy, then 13-½ months old, announced from the head of the stairs, *"We don't want another baby here!"*]

When he was 14 months, Dana saw some jet trails way up near

the clouds and said, "Look at airplane scratching sky!" Coming into our den, while I was playing the death scene in Boris Godunov on the record player, he went up to the speaker, patted it and said, "Poor man. Don't cry, man." Dana was also very bright mechanically and, even at 14 months, he could take things apart — like his toys — and put them back together almost perfectly.

As an adult, after taking a number of courses in physics, chemistry and mathematics, and graduating with a 4.0 average, Dana told me he wanted to become a medical laboratory technician. I countered with, "Dana, you are brighter than 99.9% of doctors. How would you feel if doctors came into your lab and ordered you around?" He responded promptly, "Dad, you live your life and I'll live mine." I respected him thoroughly for his fierce sense of independence, a trait I see and respect in all four of my biological children – Kathy, Dana, Kevin, Carol – and in my two stepchildren Ariela (née Clara), and Johannes.

My wife Simone often fails to recognize my intense respect for independence in others. For example, in the fine movie, *Mrs. Brown,* Queen Victoria mourns incessantly for her deceased husband, Prince Albert. The Scot, "John Brown," infinitely below her station, is instrumental to the queen's recovery and in a re-emergence of her proper sense of authority. He also is forceful in helping her to assert herself. He is dedicated to her as both his queen and as a person he admires, but he minces no words in expressing his opinion as to what is best for her.

After viewing the movie, Simone said to me that John Brown was just a "macho man" (perhaps her short sight). But I disagreed with her, saying that John Brown was only attempting to do his job by helping Victoria overcome her grief and become an effective, assertive person again as Queen of England. He had also risked his life and his pride for her. He was forceful with her because he knew it was in her best interest.

Is not that the stance that a good psychiatrist or psychotherapist should have with the patient? Moreover, it is the power and authority that most everyone has to help others and themselves. I have called this "natural authority," which I see as not just a *choice,* but also a *responsibility.*

"Natural authority" has connections with Immanuel Kant's "categorical imperative" (Kant, 1949). Kant wrote that morality imposes the responsibility to behave as if your behavior was a standard for a perfect world. In part, that behavior sets an example for others to emulate. It also permits people to help the world directly. As I said above, that behavior permits people to feel good about themselves.

Kant says so beautifully, "good will is good ... in itself. Even if ... it should yet achieve nothing ... like a jewel, it would still shine by its own light, as a thing which has its whole value in itself. Its usefulness or fruitlessness can neither add to nor take away anything from its value."

That it betters our world and adds to our self-esteem are important bonuses.

"Natural authority" also applies to our behavior toward others. For example, seeing someone suffering or in danger gives you a responsibility to try to help directly or indirectly by informing police or other authorities. Endangering yourself or others in trying to help violates your responsibility to yourself, but having experience and having developed skills in helping may empower you to take that risk. Also, awareness of "natural authority" gives you the ability to respect choices others make, regardless of how incorrect they may seem to you. I had a responsibility to respect Dana's choice of occupation with good will, expressed openly and freely, without glancing sideways, rolling my eyes or repeatedly questioning his judgment by asking, "Are you sure that is what you want to do?"

## COMMUNICATION

There are many levels of communication, ranging from the clear, verbal statement of fact, down to subtle, usually ambiguous, gestures of eye-rolling, voice intonation, a shrug of the shoulders, grunts or raised eyebrows. In a robbery, if the victim asks, "Is this a stick-up," the response might be a direct and clear, "yes," or a vocal, "uh-huh;" a forward gesture with the gun; a threatening grimace; or, perhaps, a (splanchnic) appearance of uncontrollable rage, all of which convey the robber's intent. If the victim is like the nervous characters portrayed by Don Knotts, who shivers, blanches and appears ready to faint, the non-verbal cues tell the robber that there is no danger from the victim. However, a victim like Sean Connery as James Bond, who stands with eyes sizing up the robber, hands raised as if poised to strike and the general body language of a jungle animal ready to spring, gives messages to the robber to be careful.

There is no problem in reading those messages, even though they are conveyed in complete silence. However, what about the body language between a mother and her infant?

To understand the body language between a mother and her infant you must watch and listen to them both together. If mother talks sweetly, but the infant cringes and averts its head and eyes, you are tempted to question the purity of mother's sweetness and what kind of experiences have occurred earlier. First, there is the question of whether or not the physical or emotional lack of responsiveness in the infant originates in its genetic structure or was the infant damaged somehow prior to birth. Second, is there some mismatch between mother and infant that affects the nature of their interaction? Third, does the mother have some prior emotional set that affects her response to her baby? For instance, she may be totally unaware of any anger, impatience or manipulative desire in her communication, which may be there or may have been there in the past. A temperamental mother may suddenly be abusive and then become mellow, and the infant has difficulty keeping up with mother's reversal of mood.

Then, there is the opposite situation. People may be calm, not temperamental and free of any desire or attempt to manipulate others, yet they may be accused of having *ulterior motives*. This is the subject of transference in Freudian psychoanalysis. Freud said that earlier experiences often color our responses to others and offered an opportunity to change these responses through therapy and psychoanalysis. People in therapy and psychoanalysis may see these things happening with the help of the analyst and can work with the analyst to change their behavior. Clearly, then, analysts must have good will and be free of hang-ups before attempting to be tools of change in emotional interactions.

In November 1970 (King, 1970), when I was observing a ten-year-old autistic child with his intelligent and loving mother, she seemed to withdraw from him whenever he came near her, as if he were a creepy insect. Her face and head pulled back, her knees turned away and the ball and toes of her foot pulled up to avoid contact with him. She was apparently unaware of this physical response to him, although she recognized and acknowledged feeling uncomfortable with him from the time he was born. Of course, the question remained whether or not he carried some genetic trait that turned her away, or whether something in her responded that way to him from the beginning. At that moment, what I later called "bonding dissonance" was occurring right in front of me. It was the kind of reaction my theories said had occurred in the mother-infant dyad of the infant who would later become schizophrenic, except in this case it was an autistic child.

The subtleties of human communication are extremely difficult to perceive by an observer and even harder to realize when you are the communicator yourself. For example, my wife Simone often fails to communicate with me in a proper way. She should talk clearly and check by frequent eye contact to be sure I heard her and understood what she said. Sometimes, she walks away in the midst of our discussion, and neither of us knows our conclusions on the matter.

[Some years ago my frustration and anger at this finally led me to a policy in which I tried to point out to her what was occurring. I attempted to elicit some direct responses from her by saying, "Simone, please tell me what you said;" or, "Simone, please come back and listen to what I have to say;" or, "Simone, please tell me whether you heard what I said;" or "Simone, please let me know whether you want to do what I suggested."

Finally, we got to the root of the problem. It was a habit arising from her upbringing within the Korean culture.

She explained, "Women are not supposed to confront issues *directly* with a man or with older people. Not doing so is a sign of respect. Woman should *not* engage in eye contact with a man while they are talking – it is *rude*."

Due to our consistent efforts since this clarification, she has begun to show rapid enhancement in her communication skills with me and with her activities in charities.]

Years ago, in the last few months before our daughter was born, I often tapped Simone's abdomen and said, "Hi, Carol, this is your daddy!" When Carol was ready to be born, I chose to remain just outside the delivery room so the doctor would be as comfortable as possible during the delivery and the birth as safe as possible. Just after Carol was born and I saw her nursing at her mother's breast, I said, "Hi, Carol, this is your daddy!" She pulled her mouth off Simone's breast, turned to me and broadly smiled. *She had recognized my voice.* We had already communicated before she was born!

From the beginning, Carol seemed to have a special bond with me. She appeared to be blissfully happy whenever I paid attention to her. The bond with her mother did not seem as strong.

A crucial episode occurred when Carol was four. Simone had made a beautiful dress for Carol. Carol was going to her nursery school wearing just a t-shirt and shorts, but Simone was insisting that she wear the dress. Carol and her mother began to fight bitterly about what Carol would wear. Simone even accused Carol of having *bad taste*.

At that point, I interrupted to say that Carol should be allowed to make her own choice of what she wore. I explained that people have an active responsibility to find out what other people want, particularly if they are their loved ones, and out of respect and dignity for them they should try to make choices that will work out for them.

At the time, my comments were based on a lack of *communication* on the whole matter. It developed later that Carol was going off to nursery school that day for a "graduation" photo. The photos later showed Carol as the only little girl dressed in a T-shirt and shorts. All the other little girls were garbed in lovely, special clothes. She should have been wearing the dress Simone had made for her. The communication between us had been clumsy.

[My practice of psychoanalysis and psychotherapy involves adults, adolescents, children, individuals, couples, families and groups. In work with couples, including some gay couples as well as heterosexual couples, I seldom express any of my own values or judgments. However, at times, when others have asked me for my opinion on an issue, I have expressed it. In working with one couple, I wrote out the following opinions: (1) verbal and physical abuse is *not* right; (2) criticizing others for their choices is *not* useful; (3) repeating a point already made is *not* wise; (4) it is most successful in a relationship to respect and even to facilitate the wishes of the person you care for.]

Deficits in bonding occur for the following reasons. Either *the infant* has genetic or other defects which prevent it from perceiving or bonding with mother, or *the mother* (1) is dead, absent (the infant might have been in an incubator for a long period); (2) is depressed and unable to bond with the infant; (3) is not in good contact with the infant, her perceptions and interactions being cluttered or otherwise incomplete; (4) is under the influence of drugs like heroin, marijuana, alcohol or other substances; (5) is preoccupied with activities like computers, phones, television or other activities which interfere with bonding; and (6) hates the infant and verbally or physically abuses it, or else simply ignores the infant, who is not fed, changed, cleaned, or stimulated for hours and days at a time.

In my opinion, a mother's neglect of her infant is most likely to be an important part of the cause for depression. It may also contribute to the addiction to drugs, alcohol, food or other substances. It may be largely responsible for impulsiveness and strong needs for attention that result in histrionic, acquisitive, and/or disorganized behavior, but not schizophrenia.

Some years after proposing my ideas on the mother-infant dyad in schizophrenia and infantile autism, I became familiar with the work of Daniel Stern (Stern, 1982). He brilliantly demonstrated and discussed the subtleties of mother-infant interactions in a way that exactly applied to those issues. Although I was initially upset over not getting recognition for having proposed these same issues much earlier than Stern, he and his colleagues and others had done a vast amount of research to demonstrate those issues beyond a reasonable doubt.

My respect for others has served me well in several ways, the most important of which is my clinical ability. In the late 1960s, a colleague went to Europe on an extended tour and wanted me to see one of his patients in his absence. The patient was an eighteen-year- old woman, who came for her first appointment with me and asked if I was going to work with her and her mother to help her control her lesbianism. I asked her what she wanted from therapy, and she said it was to help her out in her stormy relationship with another woman. Initially, we attempted to accomplish that goal during the two sessions a week I saw her, but it soon appeared that she was not very dedicated to lesbianism. Apparently, she had been using her alleged sexual orientation to manipulate her mother and the other psychiatrist. Soon, she became interested in a young man and became very involved with him, even going to school near him on the east coast.

Almost one year later, I received a letter from her telling me how much she appreciated my having helped her to find her "true self." I do not know whether this "true self" remained heterosexual, but that is irrelevant to the more important fact that her confidence and self- esteem seem to have improved vastly since my treatment of her that summer.

Patients will test their psychotherapists to see whether they really are able to respect them. One young man of 18 was brought by his parents to me to work on him. My sincere respect for him as a person had such a strong impact that he went to work, moved out of his parents' house and began paying for his own therapy, which he continued for some years until he finally became an attorney. I understand that he now may become a judge.

[Speaking of young people, my daughter Carol told me recently that she wanted to become a physician. She had graduated from New York University and had worked in a Manhattan dermatologist's office. She had obtained her degree in history, but went to Boston to obtain a Ph.D. in English literature, having been a Shakespeare scholar and wanting to teach. However, in Boston she had worked for a gynecologist who encouraged Carol to become a doctor.

In her jobs, Carol has always been well liked, in addition to being smart and beautiful. She had tested with an IQ of around 160 and had attended a private elementary school for highly gifted children, but had taken only a few science and math courses, in which she had done quite well. She said that she wanted to become a psychiatrist and could she take over my practice when I retired. When I told her that I did not plan to retire, she managed to ask me in a diplomatic way if she could take it over if and whenever I died. I said that the relationship between a psychiatrist and a patient is so complex that taking over a psychiatric practice would be like taking over a marriage.

I believe that Carol still has a strong attachment to me and still yearns for the closeness we had when she was a little child. It makes me feel sad for her, but she does take care of herself and even asked if she could work for me. I think she recognizes her charm and intelligence and is confident that my patients could undergo an easy transition from being treated by me to being treated by her.]

A young man, age fourteen, was brought to me by his parents, who claimed that he was impossible to deal with. After several sessions in which he gradually began to trust me, he brought a knife, which he said he was planning to use to kill his parents. I offered to keep the knife to protect him from the temptation of carrying out his dangerous plan. He gave me the knife, but several weeks later asked for it back. I gave it to him, my confidence in him permitting me to feel fairly certain that he would never carry out such a plan. The following week, he informed me that he had been testing me, because he was afraid that I reported everything to his parents; this had been the ultimate test. After that, he was able to talk with me even more freely than he had before and made marvelous progress over the additional eight or nine months he was in treatment with me.

[This experience contrasts sharply with the extreme caution our current society seems to impose on therapists because of the fear of violence. I continue to use my best judgment and find that my emotions are an excellent litmus of what my patients feel and what I can expect of them.]

Further illustration is furnished by a group of inmates I saw in a group therapy session at a California prison almost three years ago. It consisted of nine inmates, six of whom were in prison for life and three of who had lesser penalties. Almost every one of them had received little respect from other members of the medical or custody staff. Most of them had been labeled "anti-social personality disorder" by many of the psychiatrists and psychologists who had examined them. I initially agreed on that diagnosis regarding one or two of them, but later changed my mind. Interestingly, all six of the "lifers" were non-white, while all the non-lifers were white.

The group members were initially extremely cautious in their comments. Often, their complaints were met with contempt by some of the prison employees, who pointed out that the inmates had no right to complain because they were responsible for their own incarceration because of their crimes. I avoided any such implications in talking with the group.

At first, the group used me as a source of information on mental illness and treatment, but gradually became more cohesive, having developed some fondness for me and more comfort with each other. After a few months of increasing cohesion and trust among the group members, one of the white men in the group was approaching parole and said there was "no way" he would ever come back to prison again. His life had changed, he said. However, the group was very critical of him for being so unrealistic. He protested by asserting his confidence in himself and for several months there was often conflict between him and the other group members about his level of "denial." Finally, his parole date came up, and with an air of deep, genuine and even tender concern, the group wished him well as he left. I sensed the tears that were welling up in the eyes of these mostly hardened criminals, who had been "macho" and resistant to any feelings of tenderness.

About one year later I received a letter from a Latino inmate who had lost all trust from the custody staff and had been repeatedly turned down for parole. He seemed to be considered the roughest, toughest, most dangerous member of the group by other staff, yet he was also the most influential with many of the inmates. I had always shown respect for him as a person. He was transferred to another prison and in his cautious, but touching, letter asked me if I remembered him. I wrote back to him that of course I remembered him, was proud of his ability to become such a valuable member of the group and wished him the best of luck. I feel confident that my response touched him and probably helped his self-esteem.

It is not difficult for me to feel respect for other people, including the inmates at the prison. Usually when they are paroled, I wish them the best of luck and sincerely mean it, even though I know, as they usually do, too, that there is a high probability that they will return. When I relate any kind of thoughts or feelings, they are genuine. If there is nothing good to say, I will only wish them the best, but if there is something good to say, I will say it, as I did with the presumably hardened criminal who wrote me. I use my feelings as a reliable guide to my choice in such matters.

I was wearing a black overcoat and a gray fedora one day as I walked by a black inmate. He said to me, "Dr. King, you is a *pimp*!" Sensing it as a compliment, I thanked him and he and several other black inmates said to me, "Dr. King, YOU DE MAN!" Because my feelings are an adequate guide, because I listen and because I generally empathize, I am very popular with the prisoners. Often, when I say to new inmates that I am Dr. King, the staff psychiatrist, they tell me that they have already heard about me and that I am a "good man." At times, new inmates come back from parole, and I will ask if they deserve to be back or if it was "bull shit." Many of them will acknowledge that they deserve it, but often they do not, especially with certain "third strike" arrests. For example, one black man was unjustly turned in to his parole officer by a neighbor. His initial arrest had been for shoplifting when he was with a relative who, without his knowledge, stole something. He and his relative were both arrested. I told him that I thought it was not fair and, with deep feeling, he thanked me. Of course he could have been lying, but I sensed that he was not. I think a major reason for his gratitude was my conveying to him my genuine belief that what he told me was true.

I have speculated that there seems to me to be an important difference in style among the three major races. Blacks originating in equatorial Africa enjoyed long days of sunshine all year and were able to see the eyes and read the expressions of others. Consequently, they seem extremely capable of "reading" others, explaining the warmth and responsiveness that seems to be a characteristic of many blacks. Being attuned to such things may make them less likely to attend to scholarly subjects and be less likely to do well on tests of formal knowledge (usually devised by white people), not because they are lacking in genetic potential, but because their attention is on the immediate input.

East Asians are descended from Mongolians dwelling on the steppes, where the sun was often low in the sky, facilitating the survival of those born with slanted eyes that naturally protected their eyes from the sun. However, slanted eyes are more difficult to "read" by others and also interfere with the full sight of the facial expressions and body language of other people. That may be why many Asians have a tendency to be paranoid. Asians may stay isolated from other people and are therefore able to study long hours and do well academically; yet their creativity may be stunted.

Caucasians are different, because they have summers with human interaction and develop the skill of reading other people to some extent; but in the winter, when it is dark and cold, they often are alone, isolated and able to reflect for months on the social and related experiences they have had. Is that why it appears that the majority of great intellectual discoveries have been made by Caucasians?

[It occurs to me that superstars in most of the sports have increasingly been black. Basketball, football, baseball, track and boxing have been dominated by black stars in the last forty years. Now, young Tiger Woods appears to be one of the world's greatest golfers, and recently, the black Williams sisters have emerged as superstars of tennis with Venus Williams winning Wimbledon just this past weekend, as I write this. That information suggests that interaction with other people, as well as the prejudice against blacks, have often distracted them from pursuing and exceeding in other endeavors.

However, it should not surprise us to see blacks pursue intellectual issues much more and with increasing success. Intelligent people do the things necessary to do. Whites having the winter to reflect and, perhaps, being threatened by the dark winter months, are keenly reminded that things change and that their lives are running out. Therefore, whites may pursue intellectual issues as a way to try to achieve some feeling of immortality. Blacks have been distracted with their ability to interact with people and lacked the motivation for scholarly pursuits. Now that appears to be changing, and blacks might also become superstars of scholasticism and science. Look at the fact that black Oprah Winfrey, through her intelligence, talent and success, has become one of the richest persons in the world.]

## POETRY AND BEAUTY

A poem I've always loved is Keats' *Ode on a Grecian Urn,* which includes the beautiful lines:

> "'Beauty is truth, truth beauty,' - that is all Ye know on earth, and all ye need to know."

Those lines inspired me to write a poem about five years ago in an attempt to present some of the ideas in *The Principle of Truth.*

# TIMETICK

## By Peter D. King, M.D., Ph.D.

Time, tick-tick away frantic action,
Whale sieving plankton, spider spin
And swallow earth, sky, cosmos.
Energy with droplet blood aspin
Pushing out in hopeful ferment
And imploding in the breast of time?
Strength, Porthos pathos, Samson strand
Arching, stretching through dimensions cubed, quadrubed,
And on point, line, plane, and cube and back with time.
Love flowing, flitting through to feel each coupling
Of mind with mind, mind and body connect and disconnect
Knowing self and heart and spirit one with other one in time.
And time: Intellect be one with time and place and other.
Love, think, feel, and therefore am and ask
And ask again, crying infant ask
Query posed in time, echoing, and asking time
"Does query make us one?" Yes one
With time, space, and on and back to point?
That with more and less and time and timelessness Infinity
will be it and its opposite

I appreciate independence and an aesthetic sense in my children as well as good health and energy. My four children have all matured to fine, loving adults with good signs of those traits.

My youngest child, Carol, loves the poems of Emily Dickinson and was inspired to write some poetry that I love. Here is a lovely poem that she wrote on February 16, 1997.

Carol D King who is Peter's daughter
Currently Carol practices Eastern medicine with Acupuncture
And soon to be P.H. d 2023

# A DAY AT THE BEACH

## By Carol D. King

The child is squatting as her hand pats the sand
like a squirrel engrossed in the tasty nature of an acorn,
the sand is the child's fortress
protecting her from all the demons of the world.
The waves caress the castle in front of the child
and she hears only distant voices of people laughing
who look like jumbled specks of colors
and the smell of dried coconut which she worships
lingers in the humidity that makes her mouth salty.
She craves to drink the thunder that the ocean produces
she would be Zuma Beach and Dr. Bob S. Johnson would realize
that she is more than a selfish princess.
She hates the smell of dried coconut.
The child ponders the day when she is a woman:
living with her children and her husband
who cooks and cleans because he is a haddad
and he would take care of their children since he cares for
their children,
who would never have *Sandpaper scars on lilies leaves*
because their adoring parents of the protective gates of heaven
would never allow harm to enter the household.
The child realizes that her dreams of love are hell
her fist crashes through the window of the castle
because she is the monster *Iron-Heart Lu*
hungry for blood, ready to get you.
The child's legs run in spirals around the castle
waiting for Doctor Bob to smother her
with his words of affection, *What's wrong with you, you ill-
forgotten child?*
If only he knew, the child is a rampant monster on the prowl
ready to go home and fall asleep.

*Adios amigo y tiene un buen vacacion!-*
The monster peels itself out of the child's body
and she is left exhausted as she falls back on the sand
and breathes in deeply
allowing the smell of dried coconut to fill her soul.

I can imagine Carol using the beach as a salty mouth that "craves the thunder that the ocean produces," but Carol's metaphor spills out so easily compared to one of my own hard-worked poems about a beach (King, 1995).

## A BEACH POEM

### By Peter D. King, M.D., Ph.D.

Laughter is on the beach.
Emotion,
That sea surface
To unplumbed depths of mind,
Rises and falls
And pushes in and out against the shore
Of other minds, other beings.
It swells and peaks,
Then fragments into laughter.
It is
A wave which swells its bulk,
Then, tripping on the sloping rise of shore,
Spills head over heels
Into foam.
Laughter is the compromise
Through which lust and violence
Transform into charm.

## SOME MORE
## CREATIVE THOUGHTS

I have had quite a number of unique ideas over my lifetime. So many of them are lost to me now — those that I failed to express in writing at the time. Here are sixteen ideas that I have recorded in my notebooks.

1.  Naugahyde used in place of leather could be mixed with a leather scent. People sniffing a jacket made out of it would imagine that it was real leather

2.  Idiopathic epilepsy could result from the chance happening that — instead of a random order in the location and discharge of brain neurons — an organized pattern begins to emerge triggering seizures. This is like a mass of troops marching in step across a bridge and causing it to vibrate violently and snap.

3.  "Ghosts" are taken seriously by many regardless of the fact that they do not exist. They represent a *task* that the living feel a need to *complete*. They symbolize *unfinished business*. If they are ignored, they "haunt," like characters in a play (as in Shakespeare's *Hamlet*) because the mission given to them through our inner minds is to affect our thoughts and behavior. When they are finally heard and their bidding has been carried out, their task is finished, and they can vanish. The haunted can finally rest.

4.  If in doubt about something, other things being equal, do that which is easier and cheaper.

5.  If you rarely make mistakes, you are being too conscientious. The percentage of your mistakes should be determined by the importance of your task.

6.  If you are not disliked by a certain percentage of people, you are being too nice. How "nice" you are should be determined by how important it is for you to be liked. It should not be overly important.

7. If an item you offer for sale sells too quickly, your price is too low. If you fail to sell only 5% of your product, your price is probably right.

8. It is natural to desire glory. It may seem desirable to you to be modest about your accomplishments, but it is better to accept credit for them. In addition to depriving yourself of honor, remaining anonymous is an act of denial that not only cheats others of the opportunity to know what really happened, but deprives those close to you of feeling proper pride in what you have done, strengthening their bonds with you and their love for you.

9. The velocity of light is limited to "c" (about 186,000 miles per second) in our universe, but perhaps it is like a pot of boiling water where a constant temperature of 100C is maintained. In other phases and other circumstances the temperature of the boiling water can exceed 100 degrees, for example, in a pressure cooker. Likewise, the velocity of light in the full expanse of reality may often exceed "c."

10. People have a basic need to comfort each other. They recognize the need of their partners to be babied by them and, in turn, to be babied by their partners. That need adds richness to their bonding and to the love between them.

11. I once came up with an example of a most ridiculous word consistent with the rules of pronunciation in our difficult English language. "FISH" can be spelled "GHOTI." Use the "gh" of "tough," the "o" of "women" and the "ti" of "ambitious." Some years later, I learned that George Bernard Shaw had also examined this sort of thing.

12. I tried to create a simplified alphabet using macrons over vowels to create two sounds for each vowel. One is the usual vowel sound, like "a" in "cat," "e" in "pet," "i" in "kit," "o" in "got" and "u" in "but." The other – with a macron over it – would

represent the sounds we make when we pronounce the letter itself, as in "late," "meet," "bite," "coat" and "boot." We then create two sounds for many of the consonants, with the macron indicating that the consonant is "voiced." Thus, for the seven pairs of consonants in the English language, "p" voiced sounds "b;" "c" voiced sounds "g;" "t" voiced sounds "d;" "f" voiced sounds "v;" "ch" voiced sounds "j;" "s" voiced sounds "z;" and "sh" voiced sounds "zh" (as in "azure"). This alphabet does constrain some of the sounds in English. Thus, "fog" would be pronounced like "fahg" instead of "fawg," but it would result in an alphabet with 19 or 20 characters and a macron.

13. Reading James Gleick's *Chaos,* I noticed that the meteorologist Lorincz wrote an article in the mid-1960s entitled "Does the Flap of a Butterfly's Wing in Brazil Cause Hurricanes in Texas?" That led me to propose that a paper may have only a *title* without any *text*. For example, "The Title of a Scientific Paper Can Obviate Any Need for Text" and "The Incredible Manipulative Ability of the Autistic Child: How Autistic Children Have Manipulated the Entire Scientific and Psychiatric Community to Believe that Autism is Caused by Chemical and Structural Abnormalities Rather Than Experiential Factors."

14. I said above that people who refuse to reveal their good actions are depriving themselves of the credit and others of the knowledge of what has really happened. They are being selfish with both themselves and others. Aristotle addressed that point when he said that philosophers want contentment and recognition, as well as truth. Further, self-deprivation makes others feel uncomfortable. Among the nicest things you can do for a person is ask her or him to do you a favor. One of the nicest things you can do for your family and friends is to do well with your own life and take good care of yourself.

15. Just now (April 11, 2000), a thought occurred as I pulled the remains of a scab off my right forearm. About three weeks ago on a Sunday, I was running the last mile of a three-mile run, veered off the walk and began to skid on the edging gravel. Knowing automatically the safest way to fall, I pulled my right arm tight against my body, rolled on my right shoulder and threw my left hand out to brake the fall. I lay still for a few moments to be sure no bones were broken, then got up and continued running. I was bleeding from my right ulnar forearm and radial elbow, my knees, my left elbow and my left palm. The bloody areas formed scabs, which healed quickly over the next two weeks or so. As the scabs began to loosen with healing, I pulled some off. I thought to myself that maybe doing that was not very smart, but I also thought of how my forced coughing and clearing my throat when I had polio may have been lifesaving.

16. It is useful to keep a clear separation between yourself and others, and between work and play, which permits you to have the freedom to have fun, not only in your work, but also in your personal relations. It also permits you to remain spontaneous, because you are emotionally responsible only for yourself. That is why I am full of energy and capable of playful good will in my work and able to be dispassionate when my children or other loved ones might do things that I believe are risky or stupid. It is clearly *their* behavior not *mine*. As a result, I almost never feel frustrated with work or upset with family members and rarely suffer from headaches and other pains. If you do not keep a clear separation between yourself and others, you risk placing on others expectations that are only your own. Perhaps it requires a strong sense of self to be capable of having such clear separation.

# CHAPTER VII
## MACHO POWER

My mother believed that "natural strength" and wholesome living made for a healthier person. I carried those ideas that she had expressed to me years ago to the limit. I used no medication or potions for colds, a runny nose, inflammation, coughing – not even for fever due to influenza – in order to develop maximal resistance to any future attacks. I also followed that policy for my children, and we all tended to be quite healthy. I had many illnesses as a child, but as an adult my last bout of influenza was for 24 hours in 1976. Since 1968, I have had only three common colds, an average of less than one cold every ten years.

However, my confidence could go too far. For instance, in Mexico and several other foreign countries, I would gradually consume increasing amounts of local water for about ten days. Then, I would drink full glasses of water straight from the tap, thinking I was safely immune from any danger. My confidence on that score was rather stupid, because of the possibility of parasite infestations and other serious consequences. I was displaying *"macho power."*

It was also my trying to be macho at age eighteen, when I went up to the topmost level of the most difficult run at Brighton, Utah, on my first attempt at skiing. Although I completely lost control of myself halfway down, I didn't break my neck.

There are other examples of my recklessness, like body surfing in winter waves on Oahu at Makaha Beach, when my back was nearly broken and surfing at "the wedge" in Newport Beach, where I almost drowned. There were some areas where I took no risks, including mountain climbing, skydiving, SCUBA diving, bungee jumping, spelunking, motorcycling or flying a private plane. I had complete taboos regarding the use of drugs, including cocaine, heroin, PSP, crack or any other that are addictive. Trying marijuana about ten times was acceptable because of my conviction that it is not addictive. I also consider myself a cautious driver. I keep fully aware of the location of my vehicle in relation to others in front, behind and beside me, and generally remain three or four car lengths behind the car ahead of me. Being courteous as a driver and allowing cars in the right position to pull in front of me also contributes to my record of never having been injured in a car and never having caused an accident. A few car accidents in which I was involved occurred only when someone else ran into me or when I was unable to avoid some minor collision.

Having survived several near-fatal illnesses and one near drowning, I have developed a good sense of caution. I do not wish to be killed or die, because I love life and wish to make the most of it. Yet, there remains some of that macho streak in me which leads me — a bit pitifully in later years — to flaunt my swimming strokes and power, run with a burst of speed, accelerate my car and otherwise engage in rather adolescent behavior.

[Note that my use of the term "macho" is a general term that could apply to men, women or children.]

By the way, I find several ranges of attitude in women: (1) those who experience and accept genuine, practical equality between men and women; (2) those who experience and seemingly accept a position of subordination to men, some of whom would probably be labeled "enablers" or "co-dependants" in so-called dysfunctional families; (3) those who experience and seemingly accept a position of subordination to men, but use their wits, wiles and wills to manipulate for advantage and power; and (4) those who do not seem to believe that real equality can exist between men and women and often appear covertly and, at times, overtly opposed to men.

My mother was an example of the first group. The second group has many examples, the most extreme of which are those women who seem to be satisfied with a life in which they are "barefoot and pregnant in front of a hot stove." The third group includes those so- called "princesses," like a woman who kept coming over to me at a party just to ask me to light her cigarette. At her third request, I handed her a book of matches and invited her to light her own cigarette. The fourth group would probably include many militant feminists.

On the Minnesota Multiphasic Personality Inventory (MMPI), the female/male scale used to skew toward a much more extreme macho attitude, in that tenderness, intimacy and expressions of feelings were scored as feminine and not masculine. On that scale, male psychiatrists happened to test high on the "female" side. As our society became much more aware of the subordination of women and was exposed to the ideas of the feminists, the proportion of men who were "female" on the MMPI increased significantly. Men became more likely to express their feelings and to seek intimacy. So, the sponsors of the test had to revise their MMPI female/male scale.

Aside from the gross anatomical differences between men and women, there may be certain personality tendencies that manifest themselves in behavior. For example, men are less likely than women to ask directions while driving to a destination. At times, when women change lanes on the freeways, they activate their turn signals long before they turn and after they turn and are likely to give a "thank you" wave after they change lanes. Men, however, are likely to activate their turn signals just as they turn and are not likely to give any "thank you" wave. In my opinion, that shows a greater tendency toward action in men and a tendency toward cooperation and willingness to depend on the generosity and accommodation of others in women. However, I think those traits cross over between the sexes by about 20%.

One of the women I dated between my second and third marriage – I'll call her "F" – was bright, independent and beautiful. She spoke to me often of the importance of self-sufficiency for women. I had great admiration for those traits in her, but was disappointed to find that she failed to practice them in her everyday life. For example, she did not take care of her automobile, letting the pressure in several of her tires drop to less than 12 pounds psi. Once, we were in a restaurant with friends, and she asked me for money to make a telephone call. When she returned, she did not give me or offer me any of the change left over and became angry with me when I asked her for it, accusing me of being "anal-retentive."

Not my mother, Ayn Rand, nor I would respond as F did because each of us would have a genuine feeling of equality and independence. F and I attended an interracial sensitivity training group in Big Sur, California, in 1972. Bill Bailey, the aggressive, black group leader, accused F of being a racist. She defended herself, claiming she was a political liberal, was non-racist and was most sympathetic to the cause of minorities, but to no avail. She ended up in tears. As the leader began to turn on me, I asked him what he meant by "racist," and he responded, "Now we are getting to the point. *A racist is someone who is not black!*"

It seems to me that F, like many other people, had certain values about civil rights and equality, but lacked the skill of applying those values in every personal situation. This may well be one origin of so- called "politically correct" behavior, where only certain values and actions are seen to be appropriate, thus interfering with the ability of a person to explore the variables.

[Having led many groups as a therapist, I find that many of the members are often reluctant to challenge or question statements made by other group members. For example, a group member, often someone with power or charisma, makes a statement the other members fail to understand. If the other group members say nothing, I may express my failure to understand what was said. Sometimes, after the statement is clarified, I ask the group members if they had understood it at first. Usually, they say, "No." They did not ask out of politeness or out of the desire not to appear stupid.

My values are different. Regardless of the situation, it is important to ask for clarification in order to have accurate communication. The issue of appearing stupid or naive is irrelevant. Accurate communication is much more important than one's image.]

There is a hierarchy of importance to various issues, with accuracy and truth, in my view, being far more important than dignity, image, reputation or popularity. However, in our society today, it seems to be the rage to appear "cool," athletic and clever (and, ideally, self-employed in one's own small business). If you don't meet most of those requirements, you might be disliked or unpopular.

One of my new patients quit my therapy treatments for that reason. She had been in therapy with another psychiatrist and had already been through many of her past feelings and experiences, but I felt it necessary to stop her occasionally to double-check what she had just said, since it was important to me to be sure of what she was saying. That caused me to appear very *uncool* and *stupid* to her.

My second ex-wife and, then, Simone, were both unhappy with that quality in me socially, especially when there was a difference of opinion. Sometimes, I express political and religious opinions that are controversial without becoming angry, without depreciating other people and without showing contempt for their beliefs. To me it seems extremely important to attempt to understand what people say and to clarify the points one is trying to make, even in political or religious discussions.

Some people seem to relish taking stupid and trivial actions solely to get a reaction from others that then lets them, in turn, blow off some hot air and appear "superior." For example, some drivers in the right lane speed up to prevent cars from merging from the on-ramp into the right lane in front of them. When someone merges anyway, the first drivers often become annoyed and honk their horns in protest. Not only are they engaging in dangerous driving by blocking the smooth merger of traffic, their honking is nothing but an annoyance and serves no purpose. Honking is to alert the other driver in case an accident might occur. Honking when it is too late is just annoying. It would be better if I ignored those actions, but I must confess that sometimes I fling my arm up in a gesture of impatience at the honkers as if to say, "Come on. Please spare us from your childish protest."

I have always been an efficient person. As an illustration, when I took my state medical boards in Illinois, I had not studied for them, having been in my internship in Michigan. Accordingly, I went to Chicago and took the first exam as fast as I could, so I could study for the next. There were about eight examinations for one and one-half hours each over a two-day period, as I recall. The longest I took for any one exam was 14 minutes and the average time was 10 minutes. I sensed when I turned in each of my blue answer books that the proctors were looking on me with increasing anger and suspicion. That my score was 74.4 and I failed the exam—passing being 75— and that 88% instead of 50% of those taking it also failed, led me to believe I had been deliberately failed because of how rapidly I had completed the exams.

That kind of treatment has happened to me on other occasions. People have informed me that what I had done was *impossible* in various endeavors, for example: (1) holding my breath eight minutes and twenty seconds; (2) doing a complete history, physical examination, drawing blood and collecting urine, doing the lab work on the blood and urine, and writing the results up completely within 29 minutes when I was a third-year medical student; and (3) doing complete psychiatric interviews within three minutes (employing a rating scale I devised for research on the comparison of several different treatment methods in psychiatry).

During my residency in 1956 in Warren, Pennsylvania, Dr. "J" and I were sent to take over the Clark-Summit state hospital. Among the residual staff physicians there were an alcoholic (who drank Scotch morning, noon and night), an alimony dodger (who worked for low wages at the hospital to avoid paying more alimony to his ex-wife and who claimed that he could "analyze any patient in five minutes") and an elderly, senile doctor whose patients would lead him by the hand to the door, take the right key from his key ring and show him how to let himself out of the locked ward. My colleague, "J," addressed the staff in a talk shortly after our arrival by opening, "It's a pleasure to meet with the staff and other patients, ah, er, I mean meet with the staff and the patients."

In another, much later, episode, I became impressed by a traffic judge in Covina, California. A plaintiff walked up toward the bench with a cowboy hat on the back of his head and a cigarette dangling from his mouth. The judge looked at him gently and without anger, wrinkled his brow and gestured with his hand in a way that said, "Please don't force me to be strict with you." The plaintiff took the cigarette out of his mouth, took his hat off, straightened up his slouch and responded to the court proceedings with appropriate dignity and respect.

This kind of appropriate, effective exercise of authority delights me. Making things work was a crucial goal and one of President Bill Clinton's best traits. Clinton was powerfully active in trying to make government work *effectively*. He would often reduce his demands to Congress in order to obtain approval of programs he felt vital to the successful conduct of this country. The opposition often used bitter- spirited tactics to block his efforts – failing to release bills from committee, failing to confirm more judges for office and, in about their worst actions, using the old smear tactic of nosing around excessively in his personal life. Clinton's sexual liaisons showed a lack of tact on his part, but they differed little from the sexual liaisons of many of our earlier presidents.

Large corporations have come to control most of the media of communication in our country and often use it to control national policy. The ever increasing absolute power of the United States has begun to chip away at our sacred liberties, and it is becoming "politically incorrect" to criticize many of our government's actions. Too many in our population seem to "bristle" at any constructive criticism of the government labeling it *"unAmerican"* to do so!

Recently, we became more concerned and actively involved with NATO in the bombing of the Serbian forces and strategic military targets in Yugoslavia. The Serbian forces and their leader had engaged in massive "ethnic cleansing" in their attempts to remove all Muslims from Kosovo. The action of the Serbs was accurately compared to the Nazi holocaust and its "ethnic cleansing" of Jews, but some writers objected to the U.S. involvement in Yugoslavia and compared it to our war in Vietnam, which involved completely different issues.

In the mid 1950s, we interfered with the election of the communist Ho Chi Min because our government knew he would get over 90% of the vote both in the north and the south. Allegedly, out of our rabid fear of communism, we permitted the South Vietnam president to declare the election *invalid,* which laid the ground for the entire conflict in Vietnam and was a major reason why so many Americans (including myself) opposed our involvement.

I believe that Vietnam would have remained in a nationalistic form of communism under Ho Chi Min, serving as a barrier to communist China, just as nationalistic communist Yugoslavia under Tito served as a barrier to communist Russia in the west. It appears to me that the political sentiment for war was not about injustice or the violation of human rights, but about *power* and *threats to power.* Our national behavior, particularly among Republicans, remains unexplained. Why did they become so unnecessarily phobic about communism? Why did they fail to recognize that Vietnam would have been an effective barrier between China and the rest of the world? Why were they willing to let the infrastructure of the United States deteriorate while spending billions of dollars of our tax money on the "defense" industry, "Star

Wars," fighting the benign use of marijuana and opposing abortion? And how many youths of our nation lost their lives?

[Many Republicans seem willing to sacrifice individual freedoms for various "states' rights," to protect power structure rather than civil rights, to increase so-called "defense" spending after the demise of the one other superpower, to grab what they can *now* at the expense of the future welfare of our population, and to prohibit the government from regulating firearms, yet scream out over the woman's right to undergo an abortion. The current *"macho power"* shown by much of our government represents a real danger to peace in the world and to human survival.]

# CHAPTER VIII
## THE ATHLETE

Both my parents were well coordinated and athletic. My mother had been a good diver, swimmer and tennis player. My father had been a star athlete and lettered in four major sports in high school. They were active with each other in sports, and both were active with me.

My father taught me to high jump, throw a ball and kick a football. My mother loved to talk with me and openly admired my good looks, good mind and athleticism. She suggested that my good qualities were partly a result of her selection of my father for his "good breeding stock." In the twenties, such ideas were common among bright young women, although my mother prided herself on her independent mind and creativity. She had an appreciation for "nature," "natural healing" and "natural strength," and had contempt for bodybuilding.

My mother's father was a fine athlete, a successful hotel and restaurant operator and a well-liked person. When she was a young lady, her father owned a big house in LaGrange, Illinois, and made a very comfortable living for his family, which allowed them to have a cook and a parlor maid. Her mother had been a child prodigy as a pianist and had performed in many concerts. It is easy to imagine that the world must have looked good to my mother and that her confidence would influence me.

Unfortunately, due to my many illnesses, I never became an

outstanding athlete as a young boy. I was pretty good at the usual sports – baseball and football and playing catch – until my illnesses began to interfere. My worst illnesses were at age four, when my temperatures spiked to 108 degrees for almost two weeks; at age nine, when scarlet fever masked my appendicitis and resulted in a ruptured appendix and peritonitis (many years before antibiotics); and at age fifteen, when I suffered three types of poliomyelitis – encephalitic (which left me with a slight tremor), bulbar (which left me with a temporary paralysis of the palette and a "hare-lip" style of speech for some years) and spinal (which caused almost total paralysis of my body and left several permanent weaknesses).

Each illness almost caused my death, but each also caused me to work extra hard to get back into top physical condition. After recovering from polio, I did pull-ups and other exercises to keep strong. I was able to compete and "letter" in swimming in high school. I also competed briefly in track, basketball, baseball and football, even while working fifteen to twenty hours a week at various outside jobs. A little later, I passed the strict physical examination for the Air Corps and went on active duty with the U.S. Army Air Forces. In those days, few people were motivated toward athletic prowess, and during basic training at Keesler Field, Mississippi, I passed the physical fitness competition, ranking third among 400 men. The war ended in Europe in May 1945, and with Japan in August, so there was no more pilot training for me. Not having the chance to become a hot fighter pilot, I wanted to go back to school. Since life in the Air Force continued with my transfer to clerk-typist school at Lowry Field in Denver, when I learned that I would be sent overseas, I decided to accept an option to enlist for one year with a bonus of almost $1,000 and a month's leave. That guaranteed my discharge after I enlisted twice – once for the duration of the war and again for one year. I served a total of just less than 21 months. Then, I was sent to Hickam Field, Oahu, and found that I loved Hawaii. I took every advantage of my spare time there after finishing my work as supply sergeant.

During my ten months in Hawaii, I was a lifeguard, a member of the Air Force Pacific swimming team, a quarterback on the Hickam Field football team, a member of the hiking club and a student in several courses. I also did much creative writing. One of my first elected courses was in psychology. Some master sergeants and several technical sergeants in the class showed resentment at my getting the highest "A," but later, some of those senior students helped move me up to the sergeant rank.

After my discharge from the Air Force, I entered The University of Chicago. At that time, I was also a member of the boy's and men's choir at St. Paul's Episcopal Church, where I joined "Gamma Kappa Delta," the Sunday night youth group. There were several attractive girls in the group to whom I immediately applied my brief *Ideal Female Requirements List.* My *List* required that her IQ must be at least 150; that she must be beautiful, sexy, strong, athletic, scholarly, assertive, liberal and feminine; and that she must fall in love and ready to be sexually free with me. I soon figured that the probability of finding all those traits in one woman was about one in twenty billion and that I had better lower my standards – at least a little. Well, that's how and where I found my first ex-wife.

My first marriage lasted 17 years (1950-1968) and produced three handsome, smart and talented children — Kathy, Dana and Kevin. My second marriage lasted but one year. I wanted to marry again – my third attempt at marital bliss — and soon was searching to find my next *ideal woman.*

My *List* was actually redundant. I failed to take into account that better human machinery may imply clusters of other superior traits. Studies of "genius" among California students many years ago found those with an IQ over 145 are generally taller, better looking, better coordinated, better students, better social beings and more likely to be successful than the average.

On August 4, 1973, I boarded my Air France 747 early and saw a beautiful "Japanese" woman on the left side of the plane. The next day in Paris, I saw her on my tour, so I checked the passenger list to see if she was married. Her name was Simone Kim. She was not married and was Korean, not Japanese. On the tour, I asked her to take my picture with my camera, and she asked me to take her picture with her camera. I asked her out to dinner that first night and from then on we were paired up.

Simone and I were married October 25, 1974, and moved into our house in Woodland Hills, California.

In March 1968, a *Reader's Digest* article on *"Aerobics,"* by Kenneth H. Cooper, came to my attention. Having been a competitive swimmer, I knew from experience how important prolonged exercise was to conditioning. In swim practice, we usually kicked for a mile, used only our arms for a mile, did repeated sprints of several hundred yards and then practiced our race strokes. A copy of *Medical World News* in the mid-'60s showed the open chest and aorta of two men who had been killed accidentally. The one who was forty years old had played football in high school, but later did virtually no exercise. His aorta and coronary arteries were half-clogged with arteriosclerosis. The other man was 78 and had been a marathon runner. His aorta and coronary arteries were almost entirely free of any arteriosclerosis, being like stainless steel pipes.

I decided that Cooper must have been trying to find the minimal amount of aerobic exercise that would give the conditioning of a marathon runner. I began to run, swim again and eventually bought a stationary bicycle in order to exercise and obtain at least 30 "aerobics points" every week. When I had worn out the stationary bike, I had a new roller put on. With it, the bike was almost indestructible, and I rode with extreme tension at an extremely high speed for thirteen minutes, four times a week. After some years of doing this along with weight-lifting with machines and free weights, my resting pulse in the afternoon would get as low as 37 beats a minute. At age 56, my oxygen uptake exceeded the levels of the most athletic 18 year-old men, and my physical condition in general continued to be excellent. I have continued those rigorous exercise routines since then.

A patient urged me to start running marathons when I was 56, and I began to run every day. I decided to do a triathlon first as part of my training. Not being sure if my joints could handle it, I ran every day and swam in 57-degree water for 1.4 miles before buying a new bicycle. The U.S. Triathlon Series in Los Angeles was scheduled for Saturday, June 25, 1983, so there were three-and-a-half months to train. At that time, I was working some 12 hours a day, five days a week. I bought a 26-pound bicycle for $346 and began bicycling for 25 miles each morning at 5 a.m., after which I ran eight miles.

After working from 8 a.m. to 8 p.m., I would arrive home and proceed to swim 1.4 miles in my unheated 57-degree pool. I continued that almost every day prior to the triathlon. Going to bed after midnight, I averaged 4 ½ hours of sleep each a night, instead of my earlier adult lifetime average of 5 ½ hours.

It happened that this triathlon was the world's largest. I won first place in the 56 to 60-year-old age group, finishing two minutes ahead of the man who won for our age group in the "Iron Man" competition four months later in Hawaii. I had been confident of winning because of my time records in practice sessions. In order to keep up my training pace for the San Francisco marathon scheduled for one month later, I ran 22 miles the day after the triathlon. That was too much too soon, and, without knowing it, I developed a stress fracture of the right femur that was not discovered until one week after the marathon. I ran the first twenty miles of the marathon well, but for the last six miles, my right leg felt like it would break off. I had to walk the last six miles, making my time of completion just over four hours.

The following year, I ran the San Francisco marathon again and finished in 3 hours and 25 minutes, which was the best time for all ages in my running club, called "The Back of the Pack," for good reason, since we were a group of mostly professional people who trained only modestly. In fact, our group's so-called "B Team" was the faster, and we won the most prizes in a variety of races in our group of three men and a woman. I was better in the longer runs, but did win many prizes for my age group in 5K and 10K races. My best times were never less than 20 or 41, respectively, but I did take five first place awards in swimming and track among men over 40 in the U.S.C. "Medical Olympics" when I was 60.

Being competitive and feeling anxious in competition, I usually avoid formal races because of the anxiety and nausea that are likely to occur. Even when the game "Pong" came out in the 1970s and I was winning against everyone who played me, including the man who allegedly invented the game, I still became nauseated during the competition. It felt as if the pace would get faster and faster with no limit until I somehow "popped."

There is not much else to say about my athletic experiences, except that I was good, but not outstanding. At twelve, I played as halfback on our football team. The opposing team's halfback, Jimmy Fuchs, happened to be outstanding and totally intimidated me. Everyone was in awe of his speed and the reckless way in which he threw his body. He began to win many athletic awards in the highest categories. At age 15, when Jimmy was 5 feet 11 inches tall and weighed 190 pounds, he ran the 100-yard dash in 9.8 seconds, at a time when Claude "Buddy" Young had set the state record with 9.6 seconds. Jimmy later won many first prizes in running and shot put. He went to Yale University and, while there, placed second in the 1952 Olympics in shot put, remarkable for a man so slender as he. He went on to win first and second place in many other world events.

Another admirable athlete was Peter George, whom I met in

Honolulu in December 1972. By that time, he was a mild-mannered orthodontist with sloping shoulders. He was about age 40, 5 feet 9 inches tall, and weighed about 165 to 170 pounds. I learned that he had been the strongest 15-year old of all time, having lifted 200 pounds plus his 148-pound weight in a military press before it was eliminated from competition. Later, he competed in the late 1940s and early 1950s, taking a number of gold medals in his weight group in competitions around the world, and either gold or silver in the Olympics.

[When I needed some new bodybuilding equipment for the gym in my house in Woodland Hills, I went down to Joe Weider's warehouse and business office on Erwin Street and bought many light weights to use with several pairs of dumbbells. The clerk who waited on me discussed "the great Peter George." He showed me the style of lifting Peter had used in competition some twenty years earlier in which Peter turned his head down and to the left side as he completed his "snatch." Peter may have been the strongest fifteen-year old on record.]

I understand that Peter George also wanted to become the *richest* man in the world and later came close to that, having leveraged some hundred million dollars in options, properties and other investments into vast wealth by the 1970s. However, a minor recession almost wiped him out. I finally met Peter through a mutual friend, Joal Cohee, M.D., a psychiatrist who later joined me in my suite of offices.

Joal Cohee had been a surfer and competed in surfboard contests in various places in California. He had won enough points each year in his age group to remain in first place for some five years. In 1972, when I was between marriages, I took an interesting woman – call her Gail – and her two children with Joal and his wife and three children to a beach house near the Kona Surf Hotel on the big island of Hawaii. The house had been loaned to me by Bill Desmond. I had made several investments in the Hawaiian Islands with Bill — William Desmond Ryan — who had formed an investment group and bought this property for its use. Bill was generous, forward-looking and kind enough to furnish lodging and automobiles as an encouragement for the investor group's "Aloha Spirit." This gave us all a home base from which to check on our investment properties, which included 400 acres on the north Kona Coast and 22½ acres of Poipu Beach on Kauai.

On a later visit to Hawaii, I went with Joal to the north shore of Oahu, where he wanted to do some winter surfing. Joal stopped at the "Banzai Pipeline," Sunset Beach, and at Haliewa, surfing many waves at each of those legendary surfing beaches. He did not surf Waimea Bay because it was not breaking (the waves must exceed 30 feet there to break), but we drove the station wagon on the dangerous dirt road around Haena Point at the northwest point of Oahu to Makaha Bay, where Joal surfed for almost an hour. Such surfing is exciting, and watching the graceful moves of the surfer through the waves is like watching a fine ballet dancer. Adding to the richness of that memory are the feel of the wind and the sound of the waves crashing on the shore.

[Joal became manic-depressive in 1971, and every few years had psychotic breaks. One time he bashed cars with a barbell as they stopped at the stop sign in front of his house, rammed a police car on the 101 freeway going 106 miles per hour, and went naked in the community of Malibu Beach with a gallon of wine, singing and drinking, in the early hours of the morning. He drowned in 1985 after he went swimming at night, following his recovery from three months of illness. Some people, including his ex-wife, thought he committed suicide, but I believe he misjudged his strength, having carefully hidden his clothing and belongings on the beach before entering the water to swim. I am sure he did not realize how much time had passed since he had been in shape for swimming. He had not swum for three months and without doubt lacked the strength he had been accustomed to. He had been caught by waves following a storm and his body washed up onto the shore four days later.]

In the spring of 1998, Simone and I spent five weeks of vacation in Singapore, Malaysia, Australia and Bali. During that time, I could swim half a mile and then run with Simone about every day. I was in fine shape, and the swimming and running were routine. Then, after about one full year of no swimming at all, I suffered several injuries to my feet and broke my left toe. I was unable to run and could only swim or use my stationary bicycle to get my minimal aerobics points. I foolishly jumped into my swimming pool that first day and proceeded to do an excessive thirty or forty laps. As a result, both my shoulders felt as if they had been broken. I had been unaware of the year passing and had acted as if I was still in top swimming shape.

[That kind of misjudgment may occur to us as we age. We may reduce our activities in the mistaken assumption that our bodies are no longer able to handle it, but it is *inactivity* that is responsible here, *i.e.,* the *lack* of sufficient exercise. We have to learn to edge back into full activity and resume exercise carefully.]

I have always enjoyed physical challenges. I would swim in the freezing waters of Lake Michigan every month of the year and run in temperatures of 116 degrees Fahrenheit in Las Vegas and Palm Springs. However, I certainly would not engage in mountain climbing, spelunking, skydiving or bungee jumping, nor ride motorcycles or fly in small private planes. The risks of those are more than ten to 35 times the risk of automobile accidents.

Simone and I enjoy running when we are on vacation in a foreign country, too. She has been a runner since 1980 and has run nine marathons so far. In fact, most of the running trophies displayed in our home are hers. When we were in Soviet Russia for two weeks in 1979, Simone and I ran for three to six miles daily, starting at about 6 a.m. We never saw another runner, except for a Scandinavian one day in Moscow. The Russians looked bent and grim as they trudged through those cold mornings on their way to work. In 1982, our same morning runs in China were totally different. Thousands of people of all ages were running in the streets or doing "I Chee" at 6 a.m. China reminded me of the U.S. in the 1930, while Russia was like the U.S. in the 1950s.

I often run several miles and never carry a bottle of water, even back when I ran as many as 25 miles. It amuses me to see people running with their fanny packs and nutrition bars, as if they were in the Sahara Desert. People who struggle with their weight all too often eat "for energy," when they would mobilize some of their fat deposits if they ate nothing at all.

Knowing when I was fifty that I had less sinew and muscle, I decided to lose five pounds and drop my weight from 155 to 150. I ate slightly less cereal and, in six weeks, lost the five pounds. I became dizzy and light-headed from hypoglycemia, but I expected it, drove carefully when it occurred and tolerated it until it stopped naturally, which illustrates how much control people can have over their bodies. It also illustrates the fact that people are quite adaptable. I am sure that we are geared to go without eating for days at a time, having ancestors who inhabited deserts, jungles, mountains and tundra, with little chance for three nice meals a day.

[Further, bottled water can be polluted by faulty cleansing at the bottling plant, failure to recycle older bottles properly or by tampering by a strange customer or a disgruntled employee.]

By keeping myself in top physical condition, I think I have somehow stimulated my immune system and other functions and become tougher and stronger. Will my immune system overcome my hepatitis C? I do not even know how I got hepatitis. I have not had a blood transfusion since I was very young and have never used any intravenous drugs. Could I have contracted it at the prison where I work? Could I have gotten it in China, Russia, Mexico or some other foreign country by ignoring some cuts, bruises or other injuries?

# Chapter IX
# Heritage and Money

## Heritage

On my mother's paternal side, my great-grandfather, William Henry Spear, Jr., was a steel mill owner who had five surviving children. His oldest child, my grandfather Harry Eldridge Spear, made a comfortable life for his family as a manager of restaurants and hotels. The next oldest was Katherine Spear. Her husband, John Evans Cornell, was the millionaire owner of the old Hyde Park Hotel on the south side of Chicago. His father had owned large stretches of land along the south shores of Lake Michigan, including East End Park and Jackson Park. I understand that he persuaded all the other owners of lakefront property in Chicago — from 67th Street on the south end all the way to Evanston on the north – to preserve a wide border of their lakefront land in perpetuity as public parkland, which later allowed for the grand string of lakefront parks running almost the entire length of Chicago.

[By the way, this reminds me of one of my early real estate actions. I tried to persuade the other owners of our 400 acres of beach property along the Kona-Kahala coast of Hawaii to donate some land as public access to the beach and to create an international marketplace nearby, which would attract the public to the magnificent open shoreline and bring them into our planned hotels and residential properties.

Unfortunately, those other owners turned against my suggestions because of the costs and possible risks.]

My grandfather's next oldest brother, William Holly Spear, became a millionaire as a major owner of the Shearson-Hammill stock brokerage firm. His younger brother Kenneth was also a highly successful businessman. The youngest child, Mary Spear, married Ralph A. Bard, the notable Chicago millionaire stockbroker who became Undersecretary of the Navy during FDR's presidency.

Others in my family who had contributed to America's early growth and prosperity included Dr. Fuller, a physician. He and his wife came from England on the Mayflower in 1620. John Hancock was a distant ancestor by marriage; his sister, Mary Hancock, married Dr. Richard Perkins, and their daughter, Lucy Perkins, married Samuel Thayer Spear in the late 1790s. John Hancock was a fine, brave man who inherited his uncle's mercantile firm. His uncle had been extremely successful; it was told that he was industrious, intelligent and a fine judge of character and eventually owned a large fleet of ships many of which traveled from England to the Colonies. As you remember, John Hancock was the first to sign our Declaration of Independence. He signed it in a grand script, large enough for King George III to read.

Another of my distant ancestors was Jeremiah Morrow, the first territorial governor of Ohio, whose granddaughter, Molly Rapier, married my great-grandfather, William Henry Spear, Jr. On my mother's paternal great-grandfather's side was the first president of the American Medical Association.

My mother's father, Harry Eldridge Spear, was a fine man and athlete. He foraged out at five each morning to select the finest produce for his restaurants; but, come one o'clock that day, he'd be out playing a game of golf. In 1913 he scored a 67, which never was beaten at his club, right up to the sale and destruction of the golf course in 1927. My father was also a fine athlete with a strong interest in electronics, in which, sadly, his professional career was sidetracked just as he finished his schooling by the ravages of the 1929 depression.

Major General Manton S. Eddie, of World War II fame, was a cousin of my maternal grandmother, Jennie Evelyn Munn Spear. She was a favorite of mine, who had been a child prodigy in music — a pianist. She gave concerts from the time she was about age ten through her early twenties. Her father, Colonel Daniel Munn, was at age 19 the youngest full colonel ever in the U.S. army. He served during the Civil War and later became a highly respected judge in Illinois. More distant relatives on that side of my family include Payson Wild, a dean at Harvard University, who also had a syndicated newspaper column.

In contrast, my father's family was not so illustrious. Admiral Ernest J. King was of note during World War II and DeWitt Clinton, a senator and governor of New York, was related through marriage by way of my great-grandfather, DeWitt Clinton King.

There were several "artists" in my family in addition to my mother and grandmother, including the ballet, then modern, dancer, cousin Grace Cornell Graff, who, with her husband, Kurt, founded the "Graff Ballet" in Chicago during the depression, stage and television actress, cousin Katherine Bard (Manulis); Aunt Kate Cornell, a wonderful Christian Science singer; and John Hancock Spear, my mother's younger brother, who was a fine singer and connoisseur of classical music.

John became an artillery officer in World War II. He and his young bride, Ester Cline Spear, appeared on the cover of the November 1942, issue of *Life* magazine bidding a loving, but sad, farewell, as he was shipping out to the European front.

Those political, athletic, scholarly, artistic and entrepreneurial family traditions affected me enormously as a young man and led me to strive to have those same qualities. My several near-fatal illnesses and my mother's loving guidance in those years also led me to feel that I had an important role to play in our society and must strive for perfection in whatever I undertook.

*Mother Jane Spear King Nationally recognized an Artist*

## MONEY

In my early youth, after I recovered from polio, my voice had a strange nasal resonance due to the soft palate paralysis. I also had a slight tremor in my hands and arms and walked with a kind of strange swagger.

Some of my high school classmates teased me rather cruelly because of those oddities, and I became increasingly uncomfortable and a little paranoid. Years later, when I was an adult, the tremor remaining from my encephalitic polio led a colleague of mine to tell the spouse of one of my patients that I was a "lush," a cruel lie which led me to paranoid feelings all over again.

As a result, I was not very social in my twenties. Studying could be done alone in privacy, and, as I pursued my education, I became increasingly interested in discovering important truths. Being wealthy, being president or being an esteemed professor were *not* my goals. I wanted to discover important truths and be recognized by the world in the company of Galileo, Newton, Shakespeare, Einstein and Freud. Although the pursuit of truth and the satisfaction of discovering some new truths were in themselves sufficient pleasure, I also had a craving for recognition.

Later, I did obtain a modest number of social, athletic and professional honors, and a few financial rewards. In addition to saving ten to twenty percent of my income, I invested in several properties in Hawaii. The first investment involved 22½ acres at Poipu Beach in Kauai. Our group bought it in 1966 and sold it in 1980 for a profit of $250,000. My share, along with proceeds from investments in several condominiums and my house in Woodland Hills, were used to buy and develop some property enjoying a spectacular view of the San Fernando Valley. I thought it might yield a huge income for me.

A builder named Al Brende and I negotiated terms on some land in Woodland Hills on which we would build my "dream house," 12 other luxury houses on "Chalk Hill" and a 120-unit apartment building on Ventura Boulevard at the base of the hill. However, one of the owners of a key parcel wanted only a 30-day escrow that we declined to accept. That deal fell through.

Jennings Engineering Company informed me that they had 15 to 20 acres of land above Sherman Oaks that we could buy for a reasonable price. On April 1, 1977, Al's brother John and I met with the owners of the land at the company's office. At an option of $2,000 a month, they offered the land to us if we took over a loan of $125,000, paid back taxes and gave them approximately $20,000, less our option payments. John said he wanted to check with his attorneys, but I nudged him and said, "John, please sign *now*."

The principal owner tragically died of a cerebral aneurysm on the golf course several weeks later, and the land might well have been tied up in probate.

Not only were we lucky to get the land, but it turned out to be 18 acres in Bel Air in the hills above Los Angeles, looking out on the west side of Los Angeles and the San Fernando Valley. We promptly began to obtain grading permits and financing to build the houses. Initially, we were planning to build a gated community with 15 houses, including Simone's and my "dream house" at the top. We were confident that our low-density plan of only 15 houses on 18 acres would be accepted, but it was forbidden because the "slope density formula" for the Santa Monica Mountains in Los Angeles would allow us to grade only *four* lots.

At that time, the U.S. had a recession and financing became almost impossible. John Brende offered to sell his share to me for cost, and I wrote him a check getting all of "Mulholland Crest" and "Kings Court" for myself.

I had formed "King Development Corporation" and was its president. Getting the necessary financing was not possible until 1985, partly because I was a practicing doctor whom lenders viewed with skepticism. All of our work on loans, insurance, permits, engineering, planning, etc., was incredibly expensive and difficult. A thick book could be written describing those experiences and another describing the vicissitudes of building four, three-million-dollar houses and selling three.

Dr. King built the French Chateau
with the community. The Kings Court
in Bel Air CA 90077

Dr. King met his wife in Paris 1972

*Dr. King build the French Chateau with community
the name after his last name, Kings Court Bel Air 90077.
Dr. King met his wife in Paris 1972*

It was more than twelve years, from 1977 until September 1989 when we moved into our "French chateau" at 3100 Kings Court in Bel Air. It had about 7,281 square feet, eight balconies, four fireplaces, two two-car garages, a basement, and magnificent views of west Los Angeles and the San Fernando Valley from its fourteen acres of land. In 1989, it could have been sold at $3.5 million. As a result, I estimated my net worth at that point to be approaching $10 million.

Alas, from 1989 on, my fortunes began to decrease. The real estate market fell apart, my medical practice declined because of the emergence of "managed care," and then, the three people who had bought houses from me in 1988, 1989 and 1990 sued me (and King Development Corporation) for "faulty construction." The latter was especially ridiculous, because my builder had done *superb* work, had been recommended by the lender and had unusually good references by many people for whom he had already built homes.

Simone had done some beautiful work on the houses, including interior designs on the fireplaces, stained glass arches above the entrance doors and floral paintings on some shutters. She even kilned some of her painted tiles for the bathrooms. We lived in our beautiful house in Kings Court for seven years.

# Chapter X

# The Psychiatrist

Today, I am a prison psychiatrist at the California Correctional Institution at Tehachapi. I remain cheerful, open and interested in my patients.

[For the first two years I worked at the Correctional Institution, I was the only doctor who never received a "602," a complaint against the staff by an inmate. Since then, I have received several "602's," perhaps because medical administrators in the state capital removed amitriptyline and other tricyclic antidepressants from the prison formulary and have forbidden their use.]

Often when I am walking through the prison grounds, inmates who know me say, "Hi, Dr. King" and may add, "He's my doctor," and "He's the greatest!" In private, some of them touchingly tell me how they appreciate my intelligent attention and wish me well. Others who see me for the first time report that they have heard from other inmates what a good person and good doctor I am. However, it is important to be firm and necessary to set limits on some inmates, who can become angry when I tell them, clearly and sympathetically, why I will not give them what they want, though some of them do apologize later for their anger at me.

Since starting to work at the prison almost four years ago, we have not had a single suicide. There are 33 state prisons in California, and I heard that we were the only one for several years without any successful suicides. Most, including ours in the past, averaged three or more a year, but in the last two years most have improved in that regard. I did wonder if it was somehow my doing, because I have had only one suicide in about 100,000 hours of seeing patients, but now I am not sure.

I am confrontational with people on some issues. On rounds in the infirmary, two of the nurses expressed strong annoyance with a patient who was admitted the previous night after voicing suicidal feelings. His manner was very demanding, and he told me he wanted another blanket because he was cold. We only give one blanket to patients on "suicide precaution," because they can tear strips of blankets and clothing to make nooses to hang themselves. We have a limited number of beds in the infirmary and try to release patients as soon as it is safe. This patient said he was not suicidal, so, "therefore," he could have a blanket. I countered that if he were not suicidal, he would be released from the infirmary. He said that if he did not get another blanket, he would kill himself.

Not being familiar with the patient because he had just entered the night before, I decided to keep him in the infirmary another day. One of the two nurses told me I was being manipulated by the patient and that I should release him from the infirmary. She and the other nurse began complaining about what babies the patients were, and how they (the nurses) wished the old days were back when the patients were not "coddled" and they could "teach them to behave themselves."

When I said to them that they seemed to be bitter about such issues, they became defensive and pointed out that the patients needed some of the discipline that must have been lacking in their upbringing. One of them cited her own strict childhood and her style of strictness in parenting her own two children, now grown up (and, I believe, dysfunctional, in that they both have serious problems with their marriages, their children, other relationships, alcohol and illegal drugs). I said that she was certainly conscientious and must feel angry towards patients who were criminals yet had the audacity to make demands. Then, I added that they (the nurses) both seemed to have trouble learning that scolding the patients didn't change their behavior, so why didn't they stop doing it.

"Something must block you from learning that many patients are this way," I said, but that only seemed to make the nurses angry with me.

I could have said nothing. I certainly guessed that my response to them would engender their anger. However, I also knew how those two nurses had caused a great deal of turmoil among the inmates in the infirmary. In addition, repeated experience has taught me that gently pointing out behavior patterns can change people, which remains to be seen here.

Relevant to changing people's behavior patterns, let me tell you about one of my private patients, who had paranoid schizophrenia. He believed that by turning in the maid of a neighbor for being a Russian spy (in about 1970), he had embarrassed CIA and FBI agents who were "moles" planted by the Russians. He believed that those agents had convinced their agencies that he was dangerous and that the agencies had persecuted him by placing him in a mental hospital and subsequently blackballed him to prevent him from working. He refused to take any psychiatric medication orally, so I gave him injections of fluphenazine decanoate (Prolixin decanoate) every two weeks, keeping him in control from breaking car and bank windows.

Because his parents would support him financially only if he cooperated with me, he accepted this regime, but expressed his fury at both them and me, indicating that he was going to kill us soon. He had a degree from a major university, had a special interest in physics and claimed that he had given the secrets of how to assemble the hydrogen bomb to Qaddafi and other terrorists in the Near East. During one of his sessions with me, he became furious and slapped my face, punched me in the chest and kicked me in the knee. I told him that he would have to leave and that I would see him two weeks later for his regular appointment and injection, but please not to attack me physically again. Being much taller and stronger than he, I was not afraid of him unless he brought a gun, and I remain alert to that possibility.

About two years later, he became furious in a session again and began to attack me physically. I told him that he would have to leave immediately. About ten minutes after leaving, he came back to my office, apologized for what he had done and said he would never do it again. Importantly, I thanked him for his promise, told him I admired his courage in coming back to apologize and said that I would continue his treatment.

[When I moved my office to my home, I was afraid to give him my new address and continued to see him at my old office by arrangement with the people who still used it. It was such an inconvenience going there just to see him that I finally gave him my home office address and saw him there for almost three years. That worked out until one day when he was late and I was with my next patient. I went to the door and told him I would have to see him another day. He was furious, screamed, threatened me with litigation, said he would kill me and told me three or four times that he was going to "torch" my house. I was out of town that weekend and afraid that he would burn down my house, so I was quite relieved on my return to find it intact. I am still fearful that he might set fire to my house and believe that seeing him at my home office is careless.]

I often wonder if my confidence and willingness to give others more chances play some role in my success. Years ago, another analyst sent me a patient, who, the analyst said, was the most difficult patient he had ever dealt with. I was glad to see the patient in psychotherapy twice a week, trying to help her with her depression, impulsiveness and frequent suicidal attempts. Since this was before antidepressants had proven so valuable, I worked with her only with therapy.

Some months after starting therapy with me, she caught herself racing her car toward a cliff, applied her brakes and swerved away from the edge, which also had happened several times before I had seen her. I decided that she had a "dissociative personality" that had taken her over and was trying to destroy her. She was totally surprised to learn this, having been totally unaware that she had a hidden self. That night, I received a telephone call from that hidden other self, who was furious with me for telling my patient about *her* existence, indicating that my action had violated *her* right to confidentiality. Much deep psychotherapeutic work was required; the patient made several later suicidal attempts; and several other psychiatrists whom her hidden self had seen had to be coaxed out of hospitalizing her.

More than a few times that kind of thing has occurred, where I have known somehow that the patient could be trusted, and it worked out. That patient finished her treatment after seven years with me and called a while ago to tell me how well she was doing. She was married, had children and was working in a responsible position that paid her more than $100,000 a year.

That kind of experience helps me have even greater trust in my intuition and also illustrates what psychology has taught – positive reinforcement works better than negative and reward works better than punishment. An important application of those concepts occurs in the "Pygmalion" effect, which demonstrated that expectations affect results. Teachers were assigned two identical groups of average students. One group of teachers was told that their students were bright. Those students did far better academically than those whose teachers were told that their students were dull. The only difference was in the expectations of the teachers (Rosenthal and Jacobson, 1968).

The importance of attitude and how easy it is to affect is illustrated by my experience after first starting full-time private practice of psychiatry in 1963. I was fairly well known, respected and quickly referred a large number of patients. I developed a waiting list within two months. When people called to make appointments or check where they were on the list, I said that they would "have to wait until June."

I would come home at night after a long, busy day, check the mail, have a martini and tell my three children (Kathy, who was then 12, Dana, 11, and Kevin, 9) to "wait until I relax." They seemed impossible to satisfy, and my waiting patients seemed annoyed with me.

Then, I realized that my responses affected their demands. So, I changed and said to my new patients, "I'll *be able* to see you in June," and their demands seemed to cease. In addition, from then on, when I came home, I would seek out my children immediately, only later sitting down to have a martini and check the mail. The children appeared much more satisfied, and their time crawling over me seemed to drop to a quarter of what it had been.

It is so important to respect the autonomy and dignity of other people and remarkably easy to convey that respect, not so much because it makes life simpler for the parent and the patient, but because it means so much in the development and maturity of the children and because a gentle, persistent approach may change people in the long run.

I recognize blockage of communication quickly and take pains to clarify it and work through the clutter with highly disturbed patients, relatively mature patients, and couples and families, as well. All seem to appreciate my ability to "cut to the chase," and progress is made fairly quickly. Not only do I address the issues that emerge in them and in their relationships outside, but I also address the issues that emerge in the relationship with me.

For example, B's parents had placed her in an orphanage at age six when her brother was born. She was devastated and became keenly aware of how many ways she had been found wanting and the many times she had been ignored by her mother. Her father was less rejecting, but seemed aloof and under the spell of her mother. B's life was spent being accommodating to her mother, who used B, but was almost never generous with her. In fact, B's mother appeared as a witness for B's brother when he unfairly sued B and her husband for large sums of money. In her sessions with me, the slightest silence on my part aroused

B's fear of my disapproval. I openly discussed this with her, pointing out the pros and cons we faced in her therapy. If I talked too much, she might fail to feel uncomfortable, and we might not have her discomfort to work with; but if I talked too little, it might damage her.

Often I ask patients what they want to do in certain situations, and, whatever their choice is, I respect it and try to abide by it. Of course, it is useful to make reference to that form of my respect for them. I have discussed it in the past, regarding therapy with highly disturbed children. Thus, a boy named "George" wanted me to be a vicious animal and not talk about "things." Instead, I used my toy telephone to talk to the animals and tell them in front of George that he did not want me to talk about him at all and that he felt uncomfortable if they were anything but vicious to him (King, 1964; King and Ekstein, 1967). That permitted me to give him information about his style of handling things and what the things were that so upset him.

Later, those issues could be connected with other things during the process of helping people become aware of hidden motives. That process changes people more quickly than psychoanalysis itself where the analyst sits behind the couch out of the sight of the patient, remains relatively incognito, and slowly connects things that occur in therapy with patterns from the past and from the present outside of therapy. I do the same thing quickly, actively and with the collaboration of the patient with whom I share the issues of technique and how we are going to proceed with therapy. Two or three sessions a week instead of four or five seem to be sufficient to accomplish the work. Sometimes, only one or two sessions a month are possible, and I am willing to do that, finding that many patients can gradually improve, even with such infrequent therapy.

After some period of months, depending on the patients, I may place them in a psychotherapy group, which is usually in addition to their individual sessions. In regard to transference, I make clear the fact that it is likely to occur and that its presence is a valuable tool we can utilize to help the patient go through a process of change, having the emotions that have caused difficulty in the past emerge in our presence for us to work on.

To me, this work is fascinating and challenging. When I first started to do it, I became exhausted and would say that I felt like a wet dishrag that had been crumpled up and tossed on the floor. With the passage of time and the acquisition of experience, I became increasingly able to do many hours of therapy without even having a break. Currently, in a typical day, I can see patients for six or seven forty-five minute sessions, take a fifteen- minute break and, then, have six or seven more forty-five minute sessions.

It is important to point out that I am a full-fledged psychoanalyst and have treated a number of patients in psychoanalysis on the couch four times a week or more. So my comparison of psychoanalysis with what I do now is based on a great deal of experience. I enjoy treating patients with psychoanalysis, but I believe that the "active" approach is better, with more frequent "active" sessions—perhaps three times a week—being best of all in permitting people to change personality.

Freud used to take his notes at the end of the day, remembering many of the details of his sessions. I have done the same thing, having an excellent memory and finding that most of the time, even with patients I have not seen for years, I remember many details of their lives and their interactions with me even without needing to consult any of my notes. However, for detailed notes, it is important to write them down immediately after the session.

The late Ralph Greenson, a psychoanalyst known and respected by the profession, was highly critical of the 45-minute hour and said it was "necessary" to have ten minutes to gather one's thoughts between patients. I found that to be unnecessary and disagree with him. It is so important to be open to individual differences and wide ranges of possible behavior, and yet Greenson—a brilliant, objective, highly trained psychoanalyst who had published many seminal articles and several books—was mistaken on this issue. Similarly, most of the psychiatric profession today has made assumptions about autism and schizophrenia and about the intellectual potential of autistic children that are wrong.

In the meetings of the psychiatric faculty at U.C.L.A. medical school, I found myself quite impatient with some of my colleagues. My colleague Arnold Mandell and I seemed so much brighter than the others on the faculty that we used to play off each other in intellectual sprints that seemed to leave the rest of them behind. The slow development of ideas and seeming close-minded style of the rest of the faculty led the two of us to develop a special bond.

In keeping with this, I have always used the minimum amount of data to reach the truth. If a difference is statistically significant, I am usually satisfied to go on to other things. Thus, in one paper, I reported a statistically significant placebo effect in schizophrenia (King and Weinberger, 1959) and saw no need to go back to discuss it because it was there for all to see. Likewise, I had studied the effects of chlorpromazine, electroshock and group therapy in schizophrenic patients (King, 1958), reaching similar conclusions to those found ten years later by Philip R. A. May (May, 1968).

May had written me for a reprint of that article and several of my others, yet never referred to it, despite the fact that our findings were almost identical. He did refer to another of my articles that touched only a small aspect of his book. I felt angry that he received so many honors and credits for his work, which seemed to me to take one issue and elaborate on it almost infinitely. He brought together several different groups who studied the subject, and, with a great deal more work and expense, reached a truth about the use of individual therapy, electroshock and chlorpromazine similar to the statistically significant results of my study of group therapy, electroshock and chlorpromazine ten years earlier. I told myself that his studies were like having 5000 nuclear missiles when 100 would be sufficient for deterrence.

I am reminded of what James Suess said about the fact that I was able to use my rating scale for some of this research in as little as three minutes for some patients. He said that it was "impossible" to do that, yet he was wrong because I was quite able to do it and even felt comfortable with those assessments that took only three minutes to complete. I am sure that he and Ralph Greenson certainly did not have "mediocre minds," yet their wrong, dogmatic positions may be what Einstein was referring to in his famous statement about "mediocre minds." Perhaps it could be restated by saying that "the rejection of possibility is the essence of tyranny."

IQ is an attempt to measure "intelligence," with 100 being average and the standard deviation being 16. One standard deviation would include about 67% of the population, with 33% being between 84 and 100, and 33% between 100 and 116. Two standard deviations would include about 95% of the population, with 2.5% being between 68 and 100, and 2.5% between 100 and 132. My IQ of 175 would be 4.7 standard deviations.

The probability of finding an IQ of 175 or above is one in 355,000 people. Among the population of almost 275 million people in the U.S., there is a probability that only 775 people could be found at that level or above, which means less than eight hundred people of all ages, both sexes and in all fields of endeavor would test that high or higher, including mathematicians, astronomers, physicists, artists, musicians, physicians, lawyers, *et al.* I understand that in addition to myself, Jerry Lewis (the comedian), General Norman Schwarzkopf (the famous general from "Desert Storm") and Quentin Tarantino (the movie writer and director) all have IQs around 175. So, making statements about what is possible for people when there are so few in the highest IQ range is risky, to which many of my own experiences are testimony.

[Imagine what a perceptive infant with such a high IQ would feel if he found "bonding dissonance" at every turn! That "bonding dissonance" may have its origins in the infants themselves is irrelevant to my existential idea that it is the connection that is important. The infants exist in this terrible bond and react to it, regardless of where it originates.]

Relevant to this is my treatment of autistic children who tested IQ in the 60s and low 70s, but appeared to have more than double that potential. One near-autistic boy of four and one-half who tested approximately 72 IQ took an eraser in my playroom, looked at it and turned it around so he could place it on the tiny blackboard ledge, a task most children under ten years old were unable to accomplish. After one year of treatment, he tested IQ 134, and his physician father wanted to stop his treatment with me. I took the father to lunch on my day off and convinced him after several hours to continue his son's treatment, which I did for another three and one-half years. In other words, there may be many people who are classified below their potential.

[When the boy returned, he ran down the hall towards me and screamed out in his unique little voice, "Dr. King, I *LOVE* you!" Four years after he had finished therapy with me, I attended his bar mitzvah. His grandmother, a tiny, elderly lady from another part of the country, came up to me, took my hand, looked into my eyes and said with her strong accent, *"Doctor King, I want you to know that **I** know just what you did."*]

His father was so impressed with me that he sent me many patients who, he thought, needed psychiatric treatment. Some years later, the boy, by then a young man, returned to see me and asked to play chess with me. He played brilliantly and rapidly, and defeated me. He looked disappointed and told me that he had thought I was the greatest chess player in the world. Then he added that I had given him one of the best games he had played in some weeks. He was a "rated" chess player at close to 1800.

Another child with classical infantile autism who had tested IQ in the high 60s and low 70s came to me at age eleven. He was able to put together jigsaw puzzles picture-side down in about one-third of the time his mother, an expert at doing jigsaw puzzles, required with the picture-side up. Several years later, he tested IQ in the high 130s and ultimately worked, married and led a life much closer to normal than any of the children treated by "behavior modification." Those other children, his mother said, were like "robots without souls." The child "had a soul," according to his mother, who saw his outcome to be the result of the warm, accepting, respecting psychotherapy I gave her son alone and, at times, with the family or her, over a period of almost six years.

On the one hand, he still had peculiarities of appearance and behavior, which were different from most people, probably as a result of physiological and structural changes in his brain either from his genetic structure or from experience during early infancy and childhood. On the other hand, my treatment of him was unique in that I did not impose myself, my language or my expectations on him in any way, except to respond directly to his questions or other communicative cues.

[A discussion of psychoanalytic psychotherapy (or "empathic therapy") in a psychiatry news article was critical of "empathic therapy," essentially on the grounds that it could stagnate and get nowhere. I disagree with this point, because I am convinced that true "empathy" will sense the patient's resistance to actually working and address that. Many times, I will "cut to the chase" with certain patients, even sometimes, though rarely, giving them direction. However, I am certainly not an impatient therapist and in my psychoanalytic training, I continued with a patient more than a year after my supervisor thought the patient was ready to stop. In retrospect, as I believe I demonstrated in the paper I wrote on the changes in that patient, I was correct to have continued his psychoanalysis. It is difficult to demonstrate such things as true, because so much intuition (art) is mixed with science in those issues. All I can do is state it here, and if there is a way of checking on me, I wrote it in an unpublished paper on "working through" in 1967, for which I received the Franz Alexander prize in the Southern California Psychoanalytic Institute.]

I was like an ethnologist who observes other creatures without interruption of their spontaneous natural patterns of behavior. That permitted the child whose mother recognized his "soul" to have no need to escape from me or repel me as I propose occurs in autistic children in infancy in what I have called "distancing" symptoms (King, 1975; King, 1978).

[Earlier today I interviewed an inmate who refused to take psychiatric medication on the grounds that he wanted to do it on his "own." After discussing the fact that a newer medication, risperidone, was almost free of side-effects, could help him concentrate and would help clear the hallucinations that interfered with his attempts to concentrate, he agreed—with obvious conflict in his pride—to take the medication. He even signed the consent form I asked him to sign. It was obvious to me that my respect for him and my explanations to the intelligent part of him permitted him to respond. That was all that needed to be done and any further comment would engender his resistance, but, to my dismay, one of the psychologists present began to talk to him like he was a child, saying, "Now you heard what Dr. King said and you will promise to carry out his instructions," etc., etc., engendering obvious resentment in the patient. I interrupted, covertly rolling my eyes at the patient to convey to him that I thought the response was baloney, saw his glance of gratitude to me, told him he could leave and thanked him for coming in. That is the kind of thing I do with people to show my respect for them and my bonding with them as fellow humans!]

There are many people, especially from lower social and economic levels, to whom abuse, separation, neglect and other dysfunctional experiences occur. They may test low on IQ tests and may have other severe gaps in their intellectual and emotional behavior, which would not occur if infancy and childhood were free of such destructive experiences. The fact that Muhammad Ali tested too low initially to be accepted by the U.S. Army may well be testimony to that phenomenon. In other words, the potential for high results in IQ testing may be far above what is observed.

Often, people recklessly claim they know "best" in an attempt to cover their tracks. In other words, they will play it safe to avoid criticism or the possibility of a lawsuit. I am highly critical of that behavior, the gist of which is presented in the following two letters relating to my profession.

### A Summary of My Comments
### At Warden Carey's Office
### On October 12, 1999

1.  In 1956, mental hospital beds peaked at one-half of all hospital beds in the U.S., and one-half of those patients were schizophrenic. Among schizophrenics who had been hospitalized four or more years, the chances of being released the next year were less than 16 out of 1,000 (Kramer, *et al.*, 1955). However, in 1956, chlorpromazine (Thorazine) was introduced in the mental hospital where I received my training, resulting in the release of 196 out of 1,000 such patients, more than twelve times the expected number (King, 1960). Beginning that year, the number of mental hospital patients dropped and continued to drop until the 1970s and 1980s, when many mental hospitals in the U.S. had closed.

2.  Psychotropics, including the most recent of such medications, require approximately one month to start to work. Not realizing that, many psychiatrists in the past raised doses repeatedly until patients were taking large amounts of such medication eventually causing many of the patients to have serious side effects, such as extrapyramidal syndromes, tardive dyskinesia, akathisia and even neuroleptic malignant

syndrome. A question among psychiatrists was whether doses large enough to cause such side effects were necessary to get benefits, and doses as large as 5,000 mg a day were given (*Proceedings, Chlorpromazine and Mental Health,* 1955). Such doses proved unnecessary and dangerous, and ultimately gave a bad image to the medication.

3. In the last five years, new atypical antipsychotics have become available. Their efficacy is comparable to chlorpromazine and other antipsychotics, but with fewer side effects. They have helped detached, socially anxious schizophrenic patients feel less discomfort and make a better adjustment to society. Since those drugs have not had years of use, it is possible that long- range side effects could emerge. Being under patent, they cost our prison as much as 100 times the cost of older analeptic medications, such as chlorpromazine, thioridazine and perphenazine.

4. Psychiatric patients compose more than 25% of our prison population, and more than 10% are in active treatment at any one time. Some of those patients are schizophrenic, but a large proportion of them have major depression "with psychosis," psychosis secondary to substance abuse and an excess of bipolar disorder. They are different from schizophrenics, who are usually paranoid, detached and often remain in poor personal contact, even after they overcome their psychotic symptoms. In contrast, those who are psychotic but not schizophrenic often become warm, responsive and even extremely close to the people they trust when they lose their psychotic symptoms. They seem to be more likely to have suffered neglect, violence and abuse in their infancy and early childhood than the "bonding dissonance" I believe to be responsible for the symptoms of schizophrenia (King, P., 1957, 1965, 1970, 1975, 1978,

1994, 1997, 1999). Giving those patients highly expensive medication designed for schizophrenia seems to be risky and an unnecessary waste of resources.

5. At times, when I was away, "contract" psychiatrists changed from medications I had prescribed to atypical antipsychotics for patients who were not schizophrenic. Those patients often complained about the change and requested me to put them back on the medication that worked so well for them earlier. Perhaps the other psychiatrists believed the patients were schizophrenic or that the newer medications were superior; or they had bought the heavy "press" of the atypical antipsychotics. However, that point illustrates the importance of diagnosis and the value of appropriate continuity in prescribing such medication. In addition it is important not to feel embarrassed or hampered in prescribing efficient doses of the medications that emptied and closed many of the mental hospitals in the U.S., especially when the patients are under close observation.

6. There is advice in Latin for doctors, *"primum non nocere,"* which means, "First, you shall do no harm." That advice is usually followed by another Latin saying, which may be, *"non forza sed arte,"* which means, "not force, but intelligent skill." I believe all of us physicians here are dedicated to those principles and all of us try to use psychotropic medication with intelligent skill. There certainly is a place for the newer psychotropic medications, but they should be used where indicated, not mindlessly.

*A Summary of My Comments*
*In My Subsequent Letter —*
*Later in 1999*

Although we had 140 hours a month of "contract" psychiatrists, often they came late or failed to come at all, left early, were unfamiliar with CCI, and usually saw only eight to sixteen patients in one day. Contrariwise, I see 100 to 200 patients, one at a time, during my now three-day week at CCI, where I work from 6:45 a.m. straight through noon without lunch until late afternoon. I am well regarded by most of the patients I see and often receive a friendly greeting from new inmates, who tell me they have heard good things about me. Since my arrival on August 26, 1996, CCI has not had a single suicide, which is evidence that we all do a good job here. As for me, in my private and public practice, I have seen approximately 100,000 hours of patients with only one suicide in 40 years.

At the prison, I routinely ask the patients what medications worked for them in the past and what medication has worked for blood relatives. In the absence of such information, I often prescribe psychotropic medication that has proven safe and effective and that costs us as little as one percent of some of the newer medications.

The stick limbs of "thalidomide babies," the "addicting" qualities of Librium in the '60s, Valium in the '70s and Xanax in the '80s, the "fen-phen" folly and the higher addicting quality of Methadone than heroin in its use to treat heroin addiction are testimony to the dangers in "state-of-the-art" medications in the past. Among recent psychotropic medications, Prozac had great press initially, but proved to have side effects and to lose its effectiveness in many patients for whom it worked initially. Depakote was considered "state-of-the-art" treatment for bipolar disorder, but research in the past two years finds it third choice, with lithium carbonate back in place as first choice. Depakote also taxes liver function, making it risky in prison populations where there is so much hepatitis. Today, side effects such as "bone" aches, bruxism, drowsiness, gastrointestinal problems, headaches, weight gain and "weird" feelings have been reported to me by patients receiving olanzapine. I hope olanzapine proves not to be dangerous, because it is so promising and, as has been written, *"appears"* to be an effective treatment for schizophrenia, a disease that certainly appears among our prison population, although a large number of our patients have major depression with psychosis, substance abuse with psychosis and an excess of bipolar disorder.

Doctors may ignore the fact that medications are a multi-billion dollar industry. New medications have patents for 17 years, giving a window of opportunity to make a fortune. Today, medical journals, advertising, brochures, audio, video, meetings for continuing medical education required to keep medical licenses valid, and even some professors and researchers on salary as "consultants" are subsidized by the pharmaceutical industry. *The New England Journal of Medicine* recently published a report on the success of a hair-growing medication without disclosing that the author was a paid consultant to the company that manufactured the product. Clearly it is unwise to assume that pharmaceutical companies resist the temptation to cheat when we see that the cigarette industry has added nicotine to its products to enhance sales and that other industries fight against protection of vanishing forests, control of pollution and reduction of damage to the ozone layer, to mention a few examples.

Our avoidance of stating those things aloud consists of a kind of conspiracy of silence in which issues are skirted, and we are put in a bind in which we are asked to watch the budget yet are damned if we do. We must spell out a policy that is clear and simple. A sample statement of policy that might work is the following:

*All inmates who receive psychotropic medication shall be monitored for side effects. Any inmates who have dangerous side effects from a medication shall not be given that medication again and must have this charted. Diligence shall be used to see that effective medications are given with the realization that it requires one month of consistent intake for most psychotropic medications to work. If an inmate fails to respond, higher doses shall be given for another month, and so on, until a maximum safe dose has been used, then a different, but appropriate, medication shall be given. The inmates being medicated shall be apprised of these issues to help them* *understand the rationale, so they have the chance to actively participate in their own treatment some day. Cost and safety of medication shall both be taken into account, and in no way shall fear of being sued be used <u>in itself</u> to justify the use of new, untried, or expensive medications. We shall accept this policy actively and without apology, with the knowledge that in itself it is a shield against lawsuits.*

Open and clear dialogue on these issues is imperative. Perhaps this letter has accomplished some of that and could serve to protect in the event of an unjustified lawsuit.

I am emphatic on the issue of accuracy and truth, because so many of the unusual things I have done or observed have been questioned. The first experience of this nature was with my mother. I found a 1913 Liberty-head nickel when I was five years old and added it to my coin collection. I told my mother about it, pointing out that allegedly there were only four of those coins in existence. Not long after that, she borrowed some coins from my collection, including the 1913 Liberty-head nickel, to pay for a five-cent loaf of bread at the grocery store. I was devastated and could not understand how she could have done that. Only later I realized that she had never really taken me seriously. Even if I was wrong about the coin's value (for example, many 1913 Liberty-head nickels were counterfeit), she did not honor my belief that it was.

Having had experiences like that has given me profound respect for the importance of respect for the "autonomy and dignity" of other people. Dale Carnegie (Carnegie, 1982) proposed that idea before and far better than anyone else, I believe. I don't think that his ideas were ever given proper credit by the psychiatric profession. I had done this with people and think most psychiatrists had, but Carnegie deserves the majority of credit. My own preconception had been that Carnegie's book was some sort of religious sales manual and would never have read it if one of my patients had not recognized that my style of therapy was so similar to the advice given by Carnegie.

Perhaps my experience with my mother and the 1913-nickel is also behind my passionate respect for the autonomy and dignity of other people. I "do unto others" in this regard, not only in my work with patients, but also in my personal relationships. The fact that few people are as careful as I in this regard has made my marriages frustrating at times, because such respect was often absent.

Recently I was going to Tehachapi to spend a Sunday night, as I usually do, because I start work at the prison at 7 a.m. Monday morning. Simone had prepared an excellent salad for dinner, and I asked her how she made the dressing. I saw that she assumed I did not trust her, instead of recognizing that I was trying to clarify the issue. Instead of answering with the recipe, she said, *"What's wrong with it?"* She reacted to my question with an adversarial, rather than collaborative, attitude.

In prisons there are two sets of employees. One set includes the service employees — the medical staff and those responsible for maintenance, counseling, psychology, psychiatry, pastoral and other services that help inmates survive in a physical and emotionally healthy way. The other set is the custody employees who provide services required to maintain peaceful, safe and secure confinement of prisoners to protect society from their crimes. Many of the inmates can be extremely violent.

Service employees are often dedicated and well-meaning people who tend to trust others and may be in danger in the presence of violent inmates. Particularly, new service employees tend to take risks with prisoners, because they are not yet aware of the harm inmates are capable of inflicting on them. Custody employees have greater authority over the operation of the prison and often must rein in the good intentions of the service staff for safety reasons, which may cause the custody staff to have contempt for the services group. Further, some of the custody staff seems to regard counseling as a waste of time that coddles worthless inmates.

After I had interviewed a disturbed, dangerous inmate, I introduced myself to a custody sergeant new to our prison. He asked me what a "peck" was. My name being "Peter," having heard some muttering about

"Peter Piper picked a peck of pickled peppers" earlier, and sensing an air of defiance in the sergeant, I was certain that he was baiting me in front of the other custody staff. Note also that the "Peter Piper" nursery rhyme ends with "if Peter Piper picked a peck of pickled peppers, where's the peck of pickled peppers Peter Piper picked?" that conveys the notion that it was empty, foolish behavior which actually accomplished nothing of merit.

I asked the new custody sergeant why he was asking me what a "peck" was. He looked sideways and said he was "just curious." I asked him why he had not looked up the meaning in a dictionary, and he said, "It's not important." I responded that it must have had some importance to him, because he had actually asked me. He said that he wanted to "drop the whole matter," but I said that now I was curious about the meaning of "peck," since I usually know the answer to most questions. I invited him to join me in getting a dictionary and looking it up, which we did.

He then seemed to enjoy looking up the meaning of "peck" and after that seemed to show respect for me and my authority. I think that experience illustrates my approach to issues that emerge from sheer curiosity to issues of my own authority, or both, and I am more diligent with other employees on that kind of issue than I am with inmates. I think that, combined with my fairness and tendency to accentuate the positive, is responsible for my administrative skill.

In my profession as a psychiatrist, the habit of defining terms and clarifying issues is extremely important. Many people in our society are sloppy in their communication and let many uncertainties continue without checking them out. I feel that it is extremely important for anyone who has a question they wish to have answered to push for a proper answer and not accept being ignored, criticized or otherwise discouraged from satisfying their curiosity, which is an issue of frustration that many children have with their parents.

Recently, China was reported to have developed the highest suicide rate of any culture in the world. China is not *supposed* to have a high incidence of depression, and when I was visiting China, I was impressed by the seemingly cheerful nature of the Chinese. They appeared to accept the various mandates of their totalitarian government philosophically and cheerfully.

Depression, like mourning, results from loss and often includes a loss of self-esteem. Frequently the loss is only imaginary. A multi-millionaire patient of mine once felt quite depressed because he felt that he had lost his entire fortune even though it had actually increased, which illustrates that even the mere *belief* that things are lost can be a major determinant of depression and even suicide.

In China, however, there really are many losses. Its population is crowded, manipulated, impoverished and has experienced severe losses, but people, except, recently, women in rural areas have remained hopeful. Earlier, women had power in the household with many children and respect as mothers. Now, however, families have usually been limited to one child. The status of being a mother has been depreciated and its duration shortened, while the suicide rate among women has mushroomed.

It would appear that the high suicide rate reflects a loss of hope among Chinese women of ever escaping from what they now see as their loss of status and the existence of bleak consequences of everyday life. Perhaps such suicide can be seen as a reasonable alternative in any context in which society undermines all feeling of hope. I do not mean to say this is actually true of China, but, rather, that it serves as a warning to that country. China offers some idealism to its people — it claims that a Marxist utopia will some day emerge.

I believe there is a growing lack of idealism these days in the U.S. Materialism seems to be the principal motivation of a majority of Americans. Our legislation, our judiciary, the media of communication, our military and even our President seem to me to be increasingly manipulated by self-serving politicians of both parties and corporate lobbying. I find the Republican Party to be more dangerous in that respect, with their attempts to limit women's abortion rights and even birth control, their opposition to laws to protect the environment and their "Star Wars" form of militarism. We threaten to become a monolithic capitalist totalitarianism in which our most important and cherished freedoms could be taken away.

There is a closely related issue among psychiatric patients — the issue of feeling trapped and at the mercy of one's surroundings. A patient I saw recently was threatened by the idea of using antidepressant medication to overcome her depression. Any kind of action she takes is a threat to her freedom. According to her mother, she was "clean" (that is, toilet trained) at six months of age and began violin lessons at the age of three years. Since childhood, she has invested any action or choice with an adversarial quality. Often, when people try to help her, she will sweep her hand through the air and say, "I'll take care of it myself." In childhood, she would do the same thing, saying only, "Myself!" She repeatedly claims that society, her doctors and her husband impose on her freedom. When she has sex relations with her husband, she has extreme resistance to any enjoyment, and the few times she has had orgasm in that context, it is brief and suddenly replaced with extreme discomfort. For her, almost every aspect of her life feels like she is compromising, and she fights against her own feeling that others are manipulating her by fighting with herself.

[In psychoanalytic terms, she has incorporated (in a primitive way) her punitive mother into her inner self (superego), which punishes her for any temptation to have pleasure. In doing this, she seriously frustrates her husband, who has become the recipient of her rage toward her father for never having rescued her from mother. Being vaguely aware of all of these vicissitudes, she hates herself for being so vindictive (like her mother).]

That contrasts with me, in that I do not fight myself and adapt rather easily to whatever I am faced with, generally seeing my actions

149

as my own choice and responsibility. I may choose things that are not easy, but blame no one else and do not even think of blaming anyone except myself.

My practice of permitting cold or flu symptoms go without relief (under my assumption that I am letting my body strengthen its ability to fight such infections) has probably built my immune system, so that I have had only three colds in the last 25 years. The last time I had flu was for 24 hours in 1976, when I baked with a fever of 104 as I flew from Boston to Los Angeles. I was afebrile by the time I arrived in Los Angeles, felt good and returned to work the next day.

However, my good health today may also be due to frequent illnesses in childhood that were in addition to the three extremely serious illnesses I have already mentioned. For years I have not hesitated to expose myself to heat, cold, moisture, or people who are sick with flu or colds, having the attitude that such exposure strengthens my resistance. Certainly, I will become vulnerable again with advancing age, but, meantime, I work, run and exercise regularly with the hope of prolonging my good health. Indeed in January 1999, after watching the Super Bowl game, my youngest son, Kevin, and I both swam in my unheated 47-degree Fahrenheit swimming pool, into which I slowly walked without flinching until I was in over my head and started swimming two laps. My example seems to have affected the behavior of my children, and they, too, are remarkably hardy, including Kathy, who is now 49 and is still surviving cystic fibrosis.

Having read what I have written, I added the "King Postulate" to my Chapter II and had several thoughts derived from it. There seems to be a gradient of ideas from truth, through maxim, axiom, postulate, dictum, idea, notion, and sentiment, to assumption and fancy, sounding like a gradient between left-brain and right-brain, (or digital and analog). Can I create a "King Axiom," a "King Notion," etc.? Perhaps parallel to the "King Postulate," I can utilize the following as the **"King Proposition:"**

"The realms of objective and subjective have been separate. However, the subjective realm has repeatedly identified something later demonstrated to be objectively true." This has occurred so many times in so many ways that no examples are necessary. However, because of the fact that subjective ideas have so often proven true, I shall state: **Every subjective notion exists in reality and is reality in some part of the extended universe - whatever that universe is....** (Reference is made here to Chapter 11, entitled "Intuition," in King, 1960.)

I am reminded of my fascination with both the large picture and the small details. I can spend hours in calculating, observing, counting and otherwise being totally captivated by whatever I find around me. Perhaps that is another reason I rarely get bored and am able to connect with so many different people. For example, at the Tehachapi prison, I saw an older-looking, heavy-set, black inmate with a cane. I noted that he had a muted sense of pride, which was almost completely disguised. Instinctively, I took his cane, which permitted him to put himself in a chair at my desk. A tiny spark appeared in his eyes, conveying that such courtesies from the prison staff were rare for him.

As we talked, I learned that he was bipolar and had been treated with both lithium carbonate and valproate in addition to other appropriate medications. I noted that he had a quick mind and said that I had found that people with bipolar disorder tend to be very quick and bright. I added that they also had a keen sense of justice and were conscientious about being fair and accurate and, indeed, would move heaven and earth to correct an injustice they had mistakenly committed toward someone else. I said to him that I had a strong hunch he was that way and that his tendency to be outspoken may well have been connected with his being in prison. He said that was true and that he dearly appreciated my willingness to even accept the possibility that he had been mostly innocent of any crime. As we talked, I learned that he had been a helicopter pilot in the Vietnam War. Later, in talking about his imprisonment, he mentioned that he had been a practicing attorney. Many other things were said in the ten or fifteen minutes I spent with him, but also important was the fact that he was like so many other people who have fascinating stories to tell. Judging not, but listening openly and respectfully, permits travel mentally to every corner of the universe.

Many strange and sometimes humorous incidents occur at the prison. One inmate had been attacked by another at work. The attacking inmate used a wide-bore metal drill to penetrate the victim's abdomen, sinking through the muscle into the abdominal cavity and veering to the left. The slippery blood spurted out, and the victim fell to the floor, where the attacker began to drill through the victim's leg bones in several places prior to being pulled off. I commented on how *lucky* the victim had been to not have had his colon or other vital organs penetrated. Then, I asked him why he had been attacked. He smiled with genuine amusement and said, as if his injury was nothing and the explanation was the most obvious possible, "I'm a crip and he's a blood."

Another patient had attempted suicide in a county prison by cutting his left arm and wrist to the bone, damaging muscles, ligaments, tendons and nerves. He had been scheduled to transfer to our prison, but was sent first to a local hospital for surgery on his wounds. As it turned out, the surgeon who would do most of the work was unable to come until the following week, so the ligaments were sutured only minimally and a cast placed over the wounds. He was returned to us to stay for several days. He became wild, pulled off part of his cast, tore out his sutures and began to pull open his wounds. I was called to the infirmary and ordered that he be given a shot of five mg of haloperidol, two mg of lorazepam and two mg of benztropine. I requested that he be left alone with the hope that he would calm down as the medication took effect, but he kept tearing at his wounds.

I did not see what happened subsequently, but it seems that the nursing staff was unable to resist the temptation to congregate around him and fuss with him. A struggle ensued, ending up with him in "five-point" restraints. He did calm down finally after that and the next morning at 7 a.m. was sitting up in bed. He cheerfully greeted me with, "Hi, doc. How're you doing?" I felt indignant about the SWAT team mentality I believed was in operation in this instance, but in retrospect I realized that several different approaches may each bring success. Generally, I find that the time to calm down is extremely important in such emergencies, especially those issues that bring out SWAT teams.

During my internship years ago, a family of children was brought into the emergency room at Sparrow Hospital. They had all ingested rat poison, and the nurse in charge was immediately eager to wash out the poison with stomach tubes. Luckily, the family had brought the carton of remaining poison, and, checking it, I found that only a tiny fraction of poison had been consumed. When I interrupted the nurse's procedure, she was furious with me, having a kind of warfare mentality that is useful during an actual emergency. She had been eager to "punish" the children for daring to get into things where they did not belong.

We were there for true emergencies, and, being one of the most active emergency services in the United States, we were often overwhelmed by the demands on us. Our task was to handle those emergencies and not to engage in some sort of educational mission of "tough love."

[I can move rapidly into action when it is clearly appropriate to do so, and, because of this, I find some seemingly "peaceful" people take offense at me. Often, they have considerable conflict about exercising authority.]

I read some articles about ancient Greece in the *Encyclopedia Americana* when I was anticipating a trip to Greece and Turkey in 1999. One statement I read there was, "While Plato totally distrusted the senses, Aristotle held them to be the source of all knowledge." (Vol. 13 [1973]: 427). That statement about Plato is not true and, again, presents an adversarial outlook on the world. Actually, Plato would agree with Aristotle, but was focusing on *sources* of input, pointing out that cave philosophers would have to depend on the data available to them, including the shadows cast by the candles, so, therefore, we must be skeptical of what is presented to our senses in our attempts to reach truth. When philosophers come out of their caves and can clearly see and measure large fragments of what they perceive, Plato, like Aristotle, would agree that we can have more confidence because we are closer to reality and better able to prove our knowledge.

It would appear that Plato and Aristotle both appreciate digital, or right brain, data. "Right brain" logic and proven knowledge may give us one view of reality, while "left brain" emotions and senses give us a slightly different view. Together, they give a more complex perception of reality, just as left and right-eye views contribute to three-dimensional vision in a synergistic way. Each view added to its counterpart is like one plus one equals three or four. Those ideas not only suggest taking time to think about what is happening before taking action, but also suggest that emotion may help to add to perception. Thus, "intuition" regarding experience may well be an important source of data.

[An appreciation of this was given in a story about Isaac Newton who had informed Edmund Halley, the English astronomer and mathematician, about one of his fundamental discoveries of planetary motion. "'Yes,' replied Halley, 'but how do you know that? Have you proved it?' Newton was taken aback. 'Why I've known it for years,' he replied. 'If you'll give me a few days, I'll certainly find you a proof of it' — as in due course he did" (Newman, J.R *The World of Mathematics.* Vol. One. New York: Simon and Schuster, 1956. 278- 279). Not being a mathematician, I have been unable to furnish the proofs needed for some my own ideas, especially those regarding the "anti-cosmon" and the "King Postulate," but someone may be able to one day - perhaps, even I.]

The motivation of the measurer should be to record objective reality, but in psychiatry today we seem to regard it as "politically incorrect" to express credit to experiential factors. For example, a recent article in a major psychiatric journal stated that older women may develop more severe symptoms of schizophrenia than men because of the influence of sex hormones, or that there may be estrogen-related forms of schizophrenia. No mention was made that a mother-girl experience in infancy may be sufficiently different from a mother-boy experience to influence symptom outcome. I sent a letter to the editor, which I am pleased to say, was published (King, 2000).

The media of communication must think news is made more exciting by polarities. In our society, adversity is believed an important ingredient to help to sell news. Testimony to this is the question often asked of me if I am a "Freudian" or a "Jungian," etc. Actually, Freud and many of the early psychoanalytic pioneers had similar points of view with only subtle differences of opinion, which may, as in the case of Plato and Aristotle, seem different only because they are viewed from different perspectives.

However, we must give the devil its due. Technology has changed our society remarkably, and the rapidity with which information is spread among the population is unbelievable. Today, we have machines in the U.S. that can outproduce the labor of any other country in the world. We have been slow to utilize that superiority, and it has been said recently that if we used it we could reverse our trade deficit. In addition, it may well be that the similarity of the market curves before the 1929 stock market crash and of 1999 are irrelevant to an ongoing growth in stock market value. The major worry is that a widespread, prolonged technical breakdown would leave people intellectually unable to function. I advocate that everyone be taught the tools to read, calculate mathematically and know the basic information necessary to rebuild the technology we possess today, just in case of a major breakdown.

# Chapter XI
## Conclusion

I n the ten chapters of this book, there has been some overlap of my experiences from the present back to the distant past, with various topics emerging without regard to the forward flow of time. This temporal and topical overlap is characteristic of dreams, thought, therapy, other interactions and even life itself. I have even conveyed the idea that such overlap is the essence of reality and even of our universe. I have deliberately refrained from reorganizing much of the material into some more traditional mold.

My manuscript also has some air of *arrogance* in it that I retain in order to present a more complete picture of myself, my experiences and my views. I have also tried to give several perspectives on each point that I make in order to approach more closely the complete truth and to do a thorough and good job of providing information about myself. The world might some day be interested in me and my thoughts. I certainly hope so. The fact that my more recent papers on schizophrenia and autism were not accepted for publication pressures me to bring them to the attention of the world and the scientific community by means of this book. Each of my unique ideas seemed so obvious and vital to me that I imagined they would be noted and accepted with accolades, which did not happen. Perhaps my annotated autobiography here will focus the world's attention on me and my ideas some day.

Am I really like my mother, who also craved fame? *Yes,* I have developed the desire to live on in history and not be just an evanescent creature that lives, dies and is totally forgotten. Does this mean that a taste of glory stimulates the appetite? Or is it the opposite in the sense that deprivation may keep the appetite active? I illustrate the latter question with two vivid "Jewish mother" jokes and what they mean to me.

Question: "How many Jewish mothers does it take to change a light bulb?" Answer: "That's difficult to answer, because most Jewish mothers would sit in the dark." The implication is that Jewish mothers take advantage of ways to dramatize their suffering. In addition, it gives them a feeling of power, even if no one is watching them.

Another "Jewish mother" joke presents more active manipulation. A Jewish man calls his mother on the phone. When she answers, she sounds weak to him, and he says, "Mother, you don't sound too good." After some back and forth, she finally says that she hasn't eaten in eight days. "You haven't eaten in eight days? That's terrible! Why haven't you been eating?" he asks. She responds, "I didn't want to have food in my mouth when you finally got around to calling me." Here, the clear implication is one of active behavior that is accompanied by the direct message that she suffers because of her son. What does this try to accomplish? Power over her son. Her behavior is geared to make him feel guilty and manipulate him into being more active in communicating with her. Even if he fails to respond to her manipulation, the mother can still have the feeling that she is exercising some element of power.

A new inmate at the prison met me for the first time and took a liking to me. He told me several jokes, including the first one above. He was rather demanding and saw me several times over several weeks, during which I told him several jokes in return. Then, on a day when I had seen him two or three times during the one week, I was busier than usual. He said he wanted to tell me something. I responded that I was extremely busy and to try to make it brief, to which he responded with a sigh, "Never mind." The next time I saw him, I pointed out to him how he was reacting to me like the Jewish mothers in the jokes and that *he* now was playing the role of martyr. He saw what he was doing and expressed his appreciation for my pointing it out. He had been trying to manipulate me in order to try to get me to change my behavior, but also to give himself some feeling of power in the context of his helplessness. It was "win-win," in that he might get my attention, but if not, at least he had a feeling that he had done something, like the person who refuses to be blindfolded at his execution by the firing squad.

It is a gesture of defiance and denial of helplessness, which has some element of recognizable power and status, as illustrated by the following joke. During his sermon, a rabbi is carried away by his own emotion. Falling on his knees and beating his chest, he cries out, "God! God! I am nothing, nothing!" The rabbi's emotion overwhelms the cantor, who also falls to his knees and beats his chest, crying out, "God! God! I am nothing!" The synagogue janitor, who is standing to the side, witnesses this emotion. He, too, is overwhelmed, falls to his knees, beats his chest and cries out, "God! God! I am nothing!" The cantor sizes up the janitor's scene, nudges the rabbi with his elbow, and says to the rabbi, "Look who says he is nothing!" The joke illustrates the awareness of the power in being a victim and the importance of status in having the right to exercise that power, even in the most humble ways.

The issues of power, manipulation and not feeling totally helpless are extremely important in cultures that have suffered from genocide, especially the Jewish culture. Centuries of pogroms capped by the Nazi holocaust, then a revival of Naziism by some "skinhead" gangs, then hearing of shootings at a Jewish school in the San Fernando Valley all continue to impress on Jews the fragility of existence and how precious each life is. No wonder the status of a child is so important, since the future survival of the race depends on the children. No wonder every method can be used to feel as if one is not totally helpless and is not at the mercy of circumstances. No wonder the development of skills that can be carried in the mind is so crucial.

People tend to want power and control, but perhaps even more than that is the desire to be understood and accepted. In "E.T.," the Steven Speilberg film, a gentle creature from outer space comes to earth and is given shelter in the home of some children. They and some of the neighbor children form a bond with E.T. and try to tell the mother about the wonderful creature in their closet. They try to get her attention as she is bringing in groceries from the station wagon in the family garage. Mother pays lip service to the children, saying things like, "Yes, that's nice, dear," and, "That's really interesting," but is preoccupied with her own needs and task. She fails to connect with the children. As a consequence, she never meets E.T. and never becomes aware that he even existed.

The movie was a "tear-jerker," which had the largest gross income of any movie ever made before it. Obviously, many people could share and empathize with E.T.'s plea for "home." E.T. wanted to go home and touched people's hearts, because so many people long for the childhood and the homes they once had or, for many, the home and the childhood they always wished for but never actually had.

It reminds me of an old fantasy that I first had at about age five. I saw myself as a visitor from outer space, who was here on earth to help people and rescue them, but they never realized what I was and what I offered. Even now, I have some of that feeling and some sadness as I write this.

The movie "E.T." generates similar thoughts and feelings to those arising from the story of Jesus Christ and the strong appeal his story has had over two thousand years to much of the world, a major part of which is the fact that God visits us by becoming Jesus. What a wonderful experience to have the *ultimate parent* come to us and understand us. A "loop of interaction" is completed when Jesus is recognized by us and we by him. Jesus joins God in heaven through the Resurrection, bringing us with him not only furnishing us with a strong sense of hope for our own recognition and eternal life but also giving us the knowledge that our innermost hearts are read, known and understood by God, Jesus and the Holy Spirit.

Absolution is offered to us by Jesus no matter who we are, nor what evil thoughts we may have had or sinful actions we may have performed. How beautiful is the idea that the closure of the circle of life ends with the very essence of acceptance that began with the birth of the innocent baby.

Those who suffer from abuse, deprivation and dysfunctional backgrounds, as well as even the most well cared-for children with ideal childhood experiences, are bound to feel some frustration, neglect and misunderstanding. It is impossible for overwhelmed parents to satisfy the infinite bundle of insatiable needs of babies and little children. Frustration is everyone's destiny but, even worse, so are illness and death. It is no wonder that "E.T." was so popular and it is certainly no wonder that Christianity appeals to the deepest spirit of so many people.

[I think that the movie "Eyes Wide Shut" also delivers a theme of childhood frustration. The hero's wife reveals to him her one-time, overwhelming lust for another man. The hero and his wife love each other, and he has been fully comfortable with their intimacy, but his knowledge of her desire for another man is infuriating and devastates him. He begins to seek a kind of vengeful sex with other women, but, regardless of a variety of incredibly lustful and dangerous temptations, his emotions and his lack of sexual focus do not permit him to actually do it. He returns to his wife, and the movie ends with the notion that their attachment and love have survived.

Although individual relationships often survive such tests, I think a deeper appeal of the movie is the parallel with the family in which infants are loved and feel themselves to be the "one and only" with mother. Later, they discover the reality that there are others who attract mother's attention and have her love, too, including father, siblings and even one or more new babies. The devastation and loss are profound, but nothing can be done; they must accept it, and life goes on. Here we can see that fear of loss and depression originate in the reality and fear of profound loss.]

It is apparent that some motivation in my writing this book is to protest against the *fear of loss*. The beginning "Preface" is about bonding with others and with ourselves, while the "Introduction" presents me as totally helpless in a hospital at age nine. It seems that *my entire life has been an attempt to deny helplessness and loneliness*, while *much of my work has been to deny the realities of loss and death*.

Regardless of what inspired me to write this book, what it says is serious and prompts me now to present another important theory that I believe *explains all psychiatric symptoms*.

## A UNIFIED THEORY OF HUMAN BEHAVIOR EXPLAINING ALL PSYCHIATRIC SYMPTOMS

**All human behavior is determined by the attempt to avoid loss. Anxiety expresses the fear of loss, and most behavior is an attempt to control anxiety. Loss of a loved person creates sadness, which may last for three to six months, while depression is the emotion of sadness that emerges from loss or a feeling of loss that includes losses within the self, such as humiliation, loss of self- respect and guilt.**

**There are two major crises in human life. The first is the gradual realization that one is not bonded to one with mother. The realization sets in that mother is a separate person, that others, such as father and siblings, also exist and that a world of other people lies outside the bond with mother. That realization is devastating, threatens with the loss of a sense of self and substance, and requires a lifetime of experience and a repertory of psychiatric symptoms to attempt to cope with it.**

**Those who escape from bonding dissonance into schizophrenia**

use schizophrenic symptoms to substitute for that loss. Those who escape from bonding dissonance physically into autistic symptoms use bonding with the non-human world with substitutive symptoms to compensate for that loss. Those who are mentally limited or become old and separated from others also use substitutive symptoms to try to compensate for that loss. Those who are deprived use a variety of symptoms, such as overeating; using drugs, alcohol, sex, and physical distractions, such as computers and TV; temperamentality; and a variety of extreme devices to try to compensate or deny that loss. Finally, those who totally lose any hope either die or become totally despairing.

The second loss is that of life itself, which begins to set in at some time after birth, but usually begins to emerge as people realize that they shall not have the children, the creations, the habits or the hope that they once had. Regardless of the struggles with death, and they are many, it inexorably approaches and overcomes. Those are the wellsprings of all of our behavior and all our psychiatric symptoms, and it is our destiny.

The issue of people having collective power is vital to another important final point. It is true that most people who are raised in a reasonably gentle, loving way by their parents will find that the "Golden Rule," the Ten Commandments and Kant's categorical imperative make sense, even before they are formally taught those guides to behavior. I have said above that dysfunctional, unprincipled, immature, self-centered people are not likely to appreciate and practice such morality. I suggested that the gradual appreciation of those moral guides will unfold with the maturation of individuals and of society, like the blossoming of plants; but this idea neglects how strong that force must be.

Think of how close Nazi Germany, the Soviet Union and Red China came to enslaving the world. Do some believe that it's possible for capitalist America to present the same kind of threat? A positive answer, reflecting our faith in God, might well be, *"No. All the tyrannies of history, despite their power, have eventually withered away."*

There has to be a stronger explanation that does not depend on divinity. Earlier, I pointed out that love and care in their earliest lives lead much of humanity to behave as if they had an inner awareness of morality. But so do villains! Do we find many people at the theater or the movies cheering for the bad guys? Didn't Lady Macbeth repeatedly try to wash the blood of the children from her hands? Obviously, there is an inner awareness of morality that in itself is not enough to explain its force.

Not only do most dysfunctional persons somehow know in their hearts the distinction between right and wrong, the rest of us know even more strongly. Although the worst tyrants are often self-tortured by the wrongs they have done, it is the myriad others who disapprove of tyranny who begin to make a difference. Morality may be genetic, but it is also learned in the crucible of time. It is sufficient to cause the eventual decline of tyranny, as we know from the testimony of history.

There are four forces in physics, the weakest of which is gravitation. A fifth force, weaker than gravitation that plays a part in the curvature of the universe, has been proposed. In "Chaos Theory," the slightest new input, such as one extra raindrop, can have a vast and profound effect over time. Yet, the force of gravitation is strong enough to hold our limitless universe within something of a boundary. I say that this is also the essence of our morality.

**Just as space permits gravitational force to curve the universe in upon itself, as shown by Einstein, so time permits moralistic force to finally manifest itself in the behavior of live beings.**

*The voice of morality is soft . . . but it is persistent.*

[Albert Einstein (Einstein, A. *Ideas and Opinions.* New York: Crown Publishers, 1954) said that society could afford to support and feed all the people on earth, should furnish a forum for all of us to communicate

165

with each other and nourish the freedom to think and create in whatever ways our fancy takes us.]

I have been lucky enough to think, create, hope, and able to communicate my collection of thoughts as presented in this book. The most important of my ideas, in the order of my awareness of them, have been: The Principle of Truth; the Hypnosis Theory of Schizophrenia; the proposal of the *i*-universe; altruism as a major drive for behavior; autistic symptoms resulting from the infant's escape from "bonding dissonance;" completion as a major motive for behavior; emotional "body-building;" "natural responsibility;" "natural authority;" intuition as a major source of truth; the King Postulate regarding the fabric of time and space in the universe; morality's origins from within us; the Philosophy of Possibility; and A Unified Theory Of Human Behavior Explaining All Psychiatric Symptoms.

I bequeath to you now all fourteen of those ideas as my heritage to humanity and my gratitude for the self-realization that permitted me to engage in this work. Just as I began this book with my gradual descent into anesthesia, so I am ending it with another such descent. The liver nodule that was supposedly benign eight months ago has proved to be malignant. Biopsy showed a hepatic cell carcinoma, which is about the size of a baseball now, yet encapsulated. If I have no metastases from the lung and bone scans I went through, then I shall have surgery. In two days I meet with my surgeon, Theodore O'Connell, and his staff, to inspect my scans and schedule surgery as soon as possible at Kaiser Foundation Hospital. I have no idea whether I shall survive, and if I do, for how long. The chances are about 50% that this surgery will cure me of liver cancer and that I shall be around for many more years. *But perhaps I will not survive....*

Regardless of what happens, please remember that I am your friend, you are my friend, and, if there is a God, he is my friend and your friend. If he exists, I certainly love him, as I know he loves me and all of us.

*I have been your voice of genius, just as you have been my voice of genius. No matter what, we are together. I am with you and you are with me and we are all part of the very structure of the entire universe... now and forever...*

## RESUME: PETER D. KING, M.D., PH.D.

**CERTIFIED:** American Board of Psychiatry & Neurology, Psychiatry 1961; Child and Adolescent Psychiatry eligible, 1963.

**EDUCATION:** *Pre-Med:* 1950, B.A., Special Honors; 1954, B.S., University of Chicago; *Medical:* 1954, M.D., University of Chicago, School of Medicine; *Rotating Intern,* E.W. Sparrow Hospital, Lansing, MI; 1954-55, *Resident,* General Psychiatry, Warren (PA) State Hospital, 1955-58 (included Special Fellow, Neurology, Philadelphia General Hospital and Neurophysiology, Eastern PA Psychiatric Institute, 1957); *USPHS Fellow,* Child and Adolescent Psychiatry, Reiss-Davis Center for Child Study, Los Angeles, California 1959-61; *Psychoanalysis,* Southern California Psychoanalytic Institute, Ph.D., 1967.

**ACADEMIC:** Assistant Professor and Assistant Clinical Professor of Psychiatry and Behavioral Sciences, *UCLA, NPI,* School of medicine, 1961-67; Associate Clinical Professor and Full Clinical Professor of Psychiatry and Behavioral Sciences, *L.A. County-USC Medical Center,* 1967; Full Instructor and Senior Analyst, Southern California Psychoanalytic Institute, 1968; *Dean,*

Training Institute, Los Angeles Group Psychotherapy Society, 1980-85.

**EMPLOYMENT:** U.S. Army Air Forces, Supply Sgt., Hickam Field, HI, 1945-47; Laboratory Associate, Dept. of Hematology, University of Chicago Clinics, 1947-54; Resident in Psychiatry, Warren (PA) State Hospital, 1955-58; Clinical Director and Dr. Research, Madison State Hospital, Madison, IN, 1958-59; Psychiatrist, Los Angeles County Juvenile Hall, 1960-63; full & part-time private practice of adult, child, adolescent, family, couple, group psychotherapy and psychopharmacology, Los Angeles, 1963-2000; Supervising psychiatrist, CA Correctional Institution, Tehachapi, 1996-2000.

**ADMINISTRATIVE:** Indiana, State Board of Mental Health Research, 1958-59; Acting Superintendent, Clark-Summit State Hospital, PA, 1956; Acting Superintendent, Hollidaysburg State Hospital, founding Director, psychiatric clinic, Altoona, PA, 1958; Medical Director, Madre de Vida Institute, Tarzana, CA 1962-63.

**MEMBERSHIP:** *Fellow:* American Psychiatric Association, American Group Psychotherapy Association, American Academy of Psychoanalysis, Southern California Psychiatric Society; *Member:* American Academy of Child and Adolescent Psychiatry, Southern California Psychoanalytic Institute & Society; *Board Member, Chair, President, etc.* of many professional organizations.

**RESEARCH BOOKS:** Approximately 50 published papers, chapters, books primarily in psychiatry; also philosophy, some published poetry. Topics include: 1) statistical comparison of different treatment methods in psychiatry, psychopharmacology, and psychotherapy; 2) basic research in schizophrenia, autism; 3) hospital administration; 4) effects of alcohol and tranquilizers on human coordination and judgment.

**HONORS:** B.A. with Special Honors, University of Chicago, 1950; Shurtleff Scholar, University of Chicago School of Medicine, 1951, 1952, 1953, 1954; Special Award, Citizens of Altoona, PA as Founder and First Director, Community Mental Health clinic, 1958; Franz Alexander Essay Prize, Southern California Psychoanalytic Institute, 1968; Poetry awards; Gold Metal, 1983, Los Angeles Triathlon; Who's Who in America, 1996—.

**PERSONAL:** Four children: Katherine, teacher and bacteriologist; Dana, medical technologist; Kevin, Ph.D., former research faculty member, University of California, Santa Barbara, now industrial chemist; Carol, N.Y.U. graduate, pursuing pre- medical education. Two stepchildren: Ariela (née Clara) Rubin, John Kim. Wife: Simone, runner, businesswoman, and U.C.L.A. student.

# BIBLIOGRAPHY

American Psychiatric Association. (1952). *Diagnostic and Statistical Manual of Mental Disorders* (1st ed.). Washington, D.C.: American Psychiatric Press.

American Psychiatric Association. (1994). *Diagnostic and Statistical Manual of Mental Disorders* (4th ed.). Washington, D.C.: American Psychiatric Press.

Bateson, G., and Mead, M. (1942). *Balinese Character: A Photographic Analysis.* New York: New York Academy. New York Academy of Sciences, Special Publication.

Bennett, E. L., Diamond, M. C., Krech, D., and Rosenzweig, M. P. (1964). "Chemical and Anatomical Plasticity of the Brain." *Science, 146,* 610-619.

Bleuler, E. (1950). *Dementia Praecox and the Group of Schizophrenias.* New York: International Universities Press.

Carnegie, D. (1982). *How to Make Friends and Influence People* (Revised ed.). New York: Pocket Books.

Dickenson, E. (1999). *Article on the Poet.* New York: New York Review of Books.

Fenichel, O. (1945). *Psychoanalytic Theory of Neurosis.* New York: W. Norton.

Ferris, T. (1998). *The Whole Shebang.* New York: Touchstone.

Freud, S. (1955). *Formulations Regarding Two Principles of Mental Functioning. Complete Psychological Works,* Vol. 12.

p. 213. London: Hogarth Press.

Gill, M. M., and Brenman, M. (1961). *Hypnosis and Related States: Psychoanalytic Studies in Regression.* New York: International Universities Press.

Goldhaber, M. (1956). *Science, 124,* 218.

Greenough, W. T., Black, J. E., and Wallace, C. S. (1987). "Experience and Brain Development." *Child Development, 58,* 539-559.

Huttenlocher, P. R. (1992). *Neural Plasticity.* In A.K. Asbury, K.M. McKahann, and W.I. McDonald (Eds.), *Diseases of the Nervous System.* New York: Saunders.

Kant, I. (1949). *Kant's Moral Philosophy.* Chicago: University of Chicago Press.

King, P. D. (1951). Unpublished manuscript.

King, P. D. (1957). "Hypnosis and Schizophrenia." *Journal of Nervous & Mental Diseases, 125,* 481-486.

King, P. D. (1957). "Anti-Matter and Parity." Submitted to *Science,* unpublished.

King, P. D. (1958). "Regressive EST, Chlorpromazine, and Group Therapy in Schizophrenics in Treatment of Hospitalized Chronic Schizophrenics." *American Journal of Psychiatry, 115*, 354-357.

King, P. D. (1959). "Phenelzine and ECT in the Treatment of Depression." *American Journal of Psychiatry, 116*, 64-65.

King, P. D. (1960). *The Principle of Truth.* New York: Philosophical Library.

King, P. D. (1960). "Chlorpromazine and Electroconvulsive Therapy in the Treatment of Newly Hospitalized Chronic Schizophrenics." *Quarterly Review of Psychiatry & Neurology, 21*, 101-105.

King, P. D. (1963). "Controlled Study of Group Psychotherapy in Schizophrenics Receiving Chlorpromazine." *Psychiatry Digest,* original article, *24*, 21-26.

King, P. D. (1964). "Theoretical Considerations of Psychotherapy with A Schizophrenic Child." *Journal of the American Academy of Child and Adolescent Psychiatry, 3*, 638-649.

King, P. D. (1965). "Schizophrenic Symptoms: Relation to Alterations of Consciousness and Wish-Fulfillment." Presented to the Southern California Psychiatric Society, Santa Barbara, California, October 31, 1965.

King, P. D. (1970). "Ego Development and the Hypnosis Theory of Schizophrenia." *Psychoanalytic Review, 57*, 647- 656.

King. P. D. (1970). Journal notes on Autism, Nov. 1970. In this book, Appendix A.

King, P. D. (1975). "Early Infantile Autism: Relation to Schizophrenia."

*Psychiatric Annals, Journal of the American Academy of Child and Adolescent Psychiatry, 14,* 666-682.

King, P. D. (1975). "The Dream as Dream Stimulus." *Psychoanalytic Review, 62,* 659-651.

King, P. D. (1978). "Schizophrenia and Its Relation to Infantile Autism." *Psychoanalytic Review, Psychiatric Annals, 8,* 342-349.

King, P. D. (1982). "The 'Giving Stance' in Psychotherapy and Psychoanalysis." Unpublished. Presented to the American Academy of Psychoanalysis, San Diego, California, December 12, 1982.

King, P. D. (1993). Personal Journal. Unpublished on biology and experience in autism and schizophrenia.

King, P. D. (1994). "Reconciliation of Biology and Experience in Profound Mental Disorders." Presented at the 16th International Congress for Psychotherapy, Seoul, Korea, August 21-25, 1994

King, P. D. (1994). "Reconciliation of Biology and Experience in Profound Mental Disorders." Proceedings, 16th International Congress for Psychotherapy, pp. 470-480, Seoul, Korea.

King, P. D. (1995). *Laughter. Songs in the Wind.* Baltimore: National Society of Poetry.

King, P. D. (1995). *Biology and Experience in Schizophrenia and Infantile Autism.* Unpublished. Used in course "Primary States of Being," Southern California Psychoanalytic Institute, 1995-97.

King, P. D. (1997). *Biology and Experience in Schizophrenia and Early Infantile Autism.* Forrest. (1996). *Best Poetry of 1996.* Baltimore: National Society of Poetry.

King, P. D. (1997). "Virtual Cosmon." Submitted to *Science*, Letters, unpublished.

King, P. D., and Ekstein, R. (1967). "The Search for Ego Controls: Progression of Play Activity in Psychotherapy with a Schizophrenic Child." *Psychoanalytic Review, 54*, 639-48.

King, P. D., and Weinberger, W. (1959). "Comparison of Prochlorperazine and Chlorpromazine in Hospitalized Chronic Schizophrenics." *American Journal of Psychiatry, 115*, 1026- 1027.

Kramer, M., Goldstein, H., Israel, R. H., and Johnson, N. A. (1955). A Historical Study of First Admissions to a State Mental Hospital, Table 11. (Public Health Monograph No. 32, Public Health Service Reports, Vol. 70, No. 11). Washington, D.C.

Laing, R. D. (1969). *The Divided Self.* New York: Pantheon Books, Div. of Random House.

Marmor, J., and Gorney, R. (1999). "Instinctual Sadism: A Recurrent Myth About Human Nature." *Journal of the American Academy of Psychoanalysis and Dynamic Psychiatry, 27*. 1-6.

Maslow, A. H. (1954). *Motivation and Personality.* New York: Harper.

Masters, W. H., and Johnson, V. E. (1966). *Human Sexual Response.* Boston: Little, Brown.

Pam, A. (1990). "Part I: Errors in Methodology. Part II: Errors in Conception." *Acta Psychiatrica Scandinavica*, Supplement, *82*, 1-35.

Peaslee, D. C. (1956). *Science, 124*, 1292.

Rakow, R. W. (1994). "Psychiatry in the Decade of the Brain."

Personal communication circulated to Members, American Academy of Psychoanalysis.

Ritzer, G. (2000). *Classical Sociological Theory.* New York: McGraw-Hill Higher Education.

Rodberg, L. S., and Weisskopf, V. F. (1957). *Science, 125,* 627.

Rosenthal, R., and Jacobson, L. (1968). *Pygmalion in the Classroom: Teacher Expectation and Pupils' Intellectual Development.* New York: Holt, Rinehart, and Winston.

Spurling, C., and King, P. D. (1954). "Studies on Thromboplastin Generation." *Journal of Laboratory & Clinical Medicine, 44,* 336-348.

Spurling, C., and King, P. D. (1954). "Studies on Thromboplastin Generation." *Reports of the Argonne Cancer Research Hospital,* Vol. 1.

Stern, D. (1982). *Affect Attunment.* New York: Free Press.

Wiesel, T. N., and Hubel, D. H. (1963). "Single Cell Responses in Striata Cortex of Kittens Deprived of Vision in One Eye." *Journal of Neurophysiology, 26,* 1003-1017.

# ABOUT THE AUTHOR

*Reader's Digest* used to have a monthly article about the most unforgettable person ever met. For me, Peter King was the one. Peter was a brilliant man, a psychiatrist and psychoanalyst (teacher and practitioner), a remarkably innovative thinker and philosopher, a superb athlete, a wonderful parent for his children and a profound parent figure for his patients. His message was compatible with the human potentials movement with its emphasis on self-actualization, and included a subtle and gracious spirituality. He lived and taught the mind-body relationship by exercising, always exercising, the mind (brutally honest self-examination) and body (marathons, triathlons, *et al.*!). I have become utterly convinced that in terms of a concise life-message and instructions for self-fulfillment, it doesn't get any better than this. I hope that readers will get a sense of scope of the man, the range of his interests, and the fascinating and important ideas he shares with us all.

www.ingramcontent.com/pod-product-compliance
Lightning Source LLC
Chambersburg PA
CBHW030247130626
46549CB00002B/422